National 5
& Higher
Geography

How to Pass Assignments

CW00927218

GRAPHY DEPT.
D.S.M.C.

NATIONAL 5 & HIGHER
Geography

Susie Clarke

HODDER
GIBSON
AN HACHETTE UK COMPANY

The Publishers would like to thank the following for permission to reproduce copyright material:

Ordnance Survey maps on pages 13–14, 48–49, 65–66, 83, 128, 145 are reproduced by permission © Crown copyright 2017. Ordnance Survey Licence number 100047450.

Ordnance Survey maps in online-only material, pages 1–2, 7, 21, 27, 39 are reproduced by permission © Crown copyright 2017. Ordnance Survey Licence number 100047450.

Maps on page 111 (and pages 17 and 21 of online-only material) © OpenStreetMap Contributors (data available under the Open Database License; see: www.openstreetmap.org/copyright)

Maps on p.119 © Google

Photo credits: p.19 © 2017 Google; **p.23** © John Goulter/Alamy Stock Photo; **p.66 (p.2** – online material) all photos © Susie Clarke; **p.94** (from top) cirrus image © Alex Yeung – Fotolia; cirrocumulus image © WILDLIFE GmbH/Alamy Stock Photo; cirrostratus image © Iain MacDiarmid/Alamy Stock Photo; altocumulus image © alybaba – Shutterstock; altostratus image © ESPY Photography/Alamy Stock Photo; nimbostratus image © Silvan Wick-natural history/Alamy Stock Photo; stratocumulus image © Mike Spence/Alamy Stock Photo; stratus image © Frank Hough/Alamy Stock Photo; cumulus image © Ed Buziak/Alamy Stock Photo; cumulonimbus image © Paul Mayall/Alamy Stock Photo; **p.111 (p.18** – online material) © Susie Clarke; **p.138 (p.33** – online material) top © Campsie News/Alamy Stock Photo; left © PictureScotland/Alamy Stock Photo; right © grough.co.uk/Alamy Stock Photo.

Although every effort has been made to ensure that website addresses are correct at time of going to press, Hodder Gibson cannot be held responsible for the content of any website mentioned in this book. It is sometimes possible to find a relocated web page by typing in the address of the home page for a website in the URL window of your browser.

Hachette UK's policy is to use papers that are natural, renewable and recyclable products and made from wood grown in sustainable forests. The logging and manufacturing processes are expected to conform to the environmental regulations of the country of origin.

Orders: please contact Bookpoint Ltd, 130 Park Drive, Milton Park, Abingdon, Oxon OX14 4SE. Telephone: (44) 01235 827720.

Fax: (44) 01235 400454. Lines are open 9.00–5.00, Monday to Saturday, with a 24-hour message answering service.

Visit our website at www.hoddereducation.co.uk. Hodder Gibson can be contacted direct on: Tel: 0141 333 4650; Fax: 0141 404 8188; email: hoddergibson@hodder.co.uk

© Susie Clarke, 2017

First published in 2017 by
Hodder Gibson, an imprint of Hodder Education,
An Hachette UK Company
211 St Vincent Street
Glasgow G2 5QY

Impression number	5 4 3 2 1
Year	2021 2020 2019 2018 2017

Cover photo © Superstock/Alamy Stock Photo

Illustrations by Aptara Inc.

Typeset in Cronos Pro Light 13/15 pts by Aptara, Inc.

Printed in Spain

A catalogue record for this title is available from the British Library

ISBN: 978 1 4718 8308 8

Contents

Additional online example studies can be found at www.hoddereducation.co.uk/updates and extras

Introduction

This book has been written to cover the assignment component of the Scottish Qualifications Authority's National 5 and Higher Geography courses. Some content may also benefit those studying Geography at National 4 level.

The purpose of the assignment is for you to demonstrate challenge and application, by getting you to draw on and apply higher order cognitive skills, knowledge and understanding within the context of a geographical topic or issue. This may be related to areas you have studied in class, but you are free to research any topic or issue of your choice, including aspects of your local environment.

Top tip

Cognitive skills are brain skills or thinking skills. Higher order cognitive skills are more complex ones that need more in-depth thinking.

The book is structured in three sections:
- Section 1 – Fieldwork
- Section 2 – Research stage
- Section 3 – Example studies

Section 1 provides an overview of the assignment at both National 5 and Higher level. It also demonstrates the structure and breakdown of marks at each level, as well as providing assistance in choosing a topic for study. Finally, there are example frameworks for writing the assignments along with exam tips regarding the Processed Information sheets.

Section 2 contains the various gathering and processing techniques that should be used when you are carrying out the assignment, along with a chapter on useful calculations. Guidance is given on how to plan, prepare and carry out each technique and what to do with the information you have collected. This section also contains activity questions at the end of each 'technique' so that you have an opportunity to test your understanding of these skills. (They also allow teachers the opportunity to assess students' understanding of these techniques, following structured lessons, and identify where further work may be needed.)

Section 3 contains a wide variety of example studies, separated out into individual chapters. As previously mentioned, you are able to choose any topic you wish, however, many students prefer to pick a topic related to what they have already studied in class. Therefore, this book provides example studies for the eight topics covered within the National 5 and Higher coursework.

Each chapter contains:
- Things to consider before choosing your study topic
- How to collect evidence
- Gathering techniques specific to the topic (if relevant)
- Processing techniques specific to the topic
- Theory related to the topic
- An example assignment

Each chapter alternates the inclusion of a National 5 or Higher example assignment. That means, whichever is not included in the book is included online. You can find the online studies here at www.hoddereducation.co.uk/updates and extras.

Please note: for the purposes of clarity and understanding, the completed Processed Information sheets shown in the physical studies examples in this book (and online) are occasionally set across several pages, to allow you to see the sorts of charts, images and detail included in them, and to make judgements as to the kind of information you might want to include. However, it's **very important** to remember that for the exam, they must NOT exceed **two A4 sheets**.

Section 1 Fieldwork

1.1
The assignment

The assignment is an essential component of the National 5 and Higher curriculums. At National 5 level the assignment is worth 20 marks (20 per cent of your overall mark). At Higher level the assignment is worth 30 marks (33 per cent of your overall mark)*.

According to the SQA, at National 5 level 'the purpose of the assignment is to demonstrate challenge and application by demonstrating skills, knowledge and understanding within the context of a geographical topic or issue'. At Higher level, 'the purpose of the assignment is to demonstrate challenge and application by requiring the candidate to draw on and apply skills, knowledge and understanding within the context of a geographical topic or issue'.

Candidates are able to research any topic or issue that they choose on a local or global level; however, they must be able to explain and analyse their chosen topic with minimum support from the teacher.

There are two stages to the assignment:
1 research stage
2 production of evidence stage.

National 5

At National 5 level, the research stage includes choosing a topic for your study (see below), collecting evidence through fieldwork methods and audio/visual resources (including the internet) and organising and processing this information into **two single-sided A4 sheets** that can be taken into the production of evidence stage. The production of evidence stage is the write-up of the assignment under exam conditions. You will have a period of one hour during which you will be required to write up your assignment using the resources you have collected (Processed Information) during your research.

At National 5 level, you must follow a specific framework when writing up your assignment. You must:
- Describe two research methods used to collect information about the topic or issue **(6 marks)**.

*It is recommended that you check the SQA website for any updates to course information and marking allocation – **www.sqa.org.uk**.

- Describe and explain, with reference to your Processed Information, findings about the topic or issue and reach a well-supported conclusion about the topic or issue **(14 marks)**.

Higher

At Higher level, candidates also have a research stage and production of evidence stage, but within the research stage the SQA expects candidates to: 'identify a geographical topic or issue, carry out research, evaluate their research methods and sources, process and use information, show detailed knowledge and understanding of the topic or issue, analyse information, reach well-supported conclusions and communicate information'.

The production of evidence stage is the write-up of the assignment under exam conditions. You will have a period of one hour and 30 minutes during which you will be required to write up your assignment using the resources you have collected (Processed Information – **two single-sided sheets of A4 paper**) during your research.

The break-down of marks at Higher level is shown below.

- Carrying out research on a geographical topic or issue **(6 marks)**
- Use of and reference to Processed Information **(4 marks)**
- Drawing on knowledge and understanding of the geographical topic or issue **(6 marks)**
- Analysing information **(8 marks)**
- Reaching an overall conclusion, supported by a range of evidence **(2 marks)**
- Communicating information **(4 marks)**

Choosing a topic

Choosing a topic for your assignment requires careful consideration. First and foremost, you must choose a topic that you are genuinely interested in. It is far easier to research and write about something that you are keen on rather than something that you have no interest in whatsoever. Here is a checklist for choosing a suitable topic.

1. Are you more interested in topics that are human or physical?
   Human ☐   Physical ☐

2. Unless you have very good knowledge and understanding of a particular topic in the National 5/Higher curriculum, you should choose a topic that you have studied or are currently studying.

Human		**Physical**	
Urban	☐	Rivers	☐
Rural	☐	Limestone	☐
Population	☐	Glaciation	☐
Development	☐	Coasts	☐
Health	☐	Environmental hazards	☐
Tourism	☐	Climate change	☐
Trade and globalisation	☐	Impact of human activities on the natural environment	☐

3. Now that you have chosen one or two 'main' topics, try to come up with a couple of specific titles within that topic. For example, if 'Rivers' is the main topic then some possible titles could be:

   ☐ Does the speed of the river change from the upper course to the lower course of a river?

   ☐ How does the load of the river change downstream?

   ☐ Does the river become more meandering downstream?

   Fill in the details of your chosen topic and titles in the spaces below.

   Topic 1 _____
   Title 1 _____
   Title 2 _____
   Title 3 _____

   Topic 2 _____
   Title 1 _____
   Title 2 _____
   Title 3 _____

4. Thinking carefully about each of the topics and possible titles you have written above, which do you feel most excited by?
   Topic 1   Topic 2

5. What is the title of your study?
   _____

6. Write down three or four research methods that you will need to carry out for this.
   1 _____
   2 _____
   3 _____
   4 _____

7. If your assignment involves fieldwork, you will need to do the following:
   ✔ Choose a suitable site:
      • You might select an area that you are familiar with, or you might need to refer to OS maps to select a site.
      • You must make sure that your chosen site is big enough/small enough for the purpose of your study.
      • You must make sure that the site is accessible.
      • Most importantly, you must make sure that it is safe to visit this site.
   ✔ Gather all the equipment that is required:
      • River studies will need a lot of equipment (measuring tape, metre stick, tangerines, record sheet, pens/pencils, etc.)
      • Maps
      • Camera/camera-phone
      • Record sheets/blank paper for field sketches
      • Pens/pencils
   ✔ Organise and plan your trip thoroughly:
      • How will you get to the location?
      • Is the time of day important?
      • Consider the weather – some studies will be too dangerous to do in wet, windy weather.
      • How many visits to this site will you need to do?
      • Can you carry out all the investigations in one day?
      • Have you got suitable clothing?
      • Is there someone who can come with you?
      • What will you do in an emergency?

Example framework for writing the National 5 assignment

State the topic or issue you have researched

Research methods

Describe **two** research methods you used to collect information about your topic or issue.

Conclusions

For this section you must:

(i) Describe and explain, in detail, the main findings of your research.

(ii) State what conclusions you have reached about your topic or issue.

A blank Higher example framework has not been included as the onus is on Higher candidates to demonstrate their own ability to write in a structured way. However, for the purpose of this book, a suggested framework is used in the example Higher studies found in Section 3 and online. You may opt to set out your assignment differently.

Example record sheet

Name of river: ....

Date studied: ....

Weather conditions: ....

Site 1 – Upper course (repeat for every site)

Velocity	1	2	3	4	5	Average

Width	

Depth	0.0				

	1	2	3	4	5	6	7	8	9	10
A axis										
B axis										
C axis										
Shape										

Internal friction	External friction

Photograph for field sketch:

Direction: ....

Exact location: ....

Top tip ⭐

Make sure you create your record sheet before you go on your field study. This will allow you to focus on exactly what measurements/recordings you need to complete and you won't waste time on site.

1.2
Processed Information – tips for the exam

The Processed Information sheets that you can take into the exam must not exceed two A4 pages. Your Processed Information will contain your assignment, which is divided into three parts:
- Introduction and research methods
- Analysing findings
- Conclusion.

Processed Information

- Should be **no longer than two A4 pages**.
- It should include diagrams, graphs, tables, photos, field sketches and cross-sections, etc. This is your opportunity to present all of the evidence that you collected in the field that will help prove or disprove the aim of your assignment.
- Arrange your diagrams in the order you want to describe and explain them and go through them one by one.
- If your graphs are not numbered e.g. Graph 1, Graph 2, you will not be given any credit for the interpretation.
- You can include brief prompts but not detailed notes.
- Mind maps are acceptable as part of your Processed Information.

Introduction and research methods

- State what your aim is.
- Mention where and why you chose to carry out your fieldwork.
- Describe any important information at this point. For example, if you visited more than one site, remember to state where these were located.
- Choose two of your 'favourite' research methods and describe them fully.
- You will **not** be given any extra marks for describing more than two research methods at this stage, so don't waste your time!

Analysing findings

- You could split this section into two parts if you prefer. For example, you could describe your findings first and then explain each one in turn, or you could describe and explain as you go along. Choose whichever approach suits you best.
- Go through each of your diagrams one by one in the order you laid them out.
- Remember, you can mention all of your research methods at this point if you want.
- You must link your findings on your Processed Information sheets to your own knowledge and understanding of the topic or issue.

Conclusion

- This should be a detailed summary of your key findings or a detailed overall judgement about the issue or topic.
- Try to make your conclusion more than just an outline of findings. You could mention what else could have been studied or what should be studied next time to get a fuller picture of the issue.
- Evaluate your research methods and comment on whether you could improve on them or make them more accurate.

Section 2 Research stage

2.1
Collecting information

One way of collecting information is to use a questionnaire. A questionnaire is a set of questions that are designed to find out specific information on a given topic.

Questionnaires

Equipment required

☞ Clipboard
☞ Pen/pencil
☞ Question sheets

Things to consider ⓘ

Questionnaires can be given to people over the phone, by post or online, but the most appropriate way of conducting a questionnaire for your study is face-to-face.

When conducting a questionnaire face to face there are a number of things that you need to consider. Firstly, who is going to fill in the questionnaire? Are you going to ask the questions and fill in the person's answers on their behalf? Or are you going to ask them to fill it in themselves?

There are different ways of asking questions and you need to think about which approach is best for your study.

* Tick-box questionnaires: these are simply where a person is given a number of questions with ready prepared answers and they have to tick the answer box that best reflects their thoughts/opinions or is most appropriate to them.

* Word-response questionnaires: these require a person to respond orally or in writing to a question.

Secondly, you must be very clear on what the purpose of your questionnaire is. Know what your title is and the importance of these findings for your explanations. You must make sure that you produce well-thought-out questions. When choosing your questions make sure you consider the following: ⇨

⇨

1   Questions must be relevant: if the questions seem too off-topic, people will question the motives behind the questionnaire.

2   Questions must be easy to understand: if your questions are confusing and people don't understand them, they won't fill them out properly so your results will be skewed.

3   Think carefully about the wording of each question: if questions can be interpreted in different ways, you might find you don't get the results you were expecting.

4   Avoid questions that could appear personal or offensive: don't ask people how much they get paid or how well educated they are. You might need to find out this information for your study, but you will need to be more subtle in your questioning. For example, ask the person to tick a box with their age category rather than asking exactly what age they are.

5   Do not ask too many questions: people are busy and don't want to stand for ages filling in a questionnaire. If your questionnaire is tick-box style, limit the number of questions to 10–15. If your questionnaire requires word responses or sentences, limit your questions to 4–6.

6   Avoid asking leading questions: these are questions that prompt someone to answer in a certain way. For example, 'Do you believe that people desperate for water in drought-stricken countries and people dying from more powerful hurricanes are a sign of global warming?'

Finally, think about where you need to go to find out this information. Is there a specific group of people that you need to speak to or can you ask the general public? If you need to ask specific people, you may need to arrange this in advance, especially if your interviewee is a busy farmer or business owner. If you plan to ask members of the public, consider where you would be likely to find suitable people. For example, if you are asking 'What do you think of the shops and services on Kilmarnock Road in Shawlands?', then you need to be situated on Kilmarnock Road itself.

Method

- Approach every n^{th} person (decide on the value of 'n' depending on how busy the street is and the number of people you need to question).
- Don't get upset if people refuse to stop.
- Begin by explaining who you are and the purpose of your questionnaire.
- Ask all your questions.
- Thank the respondent for his/her time at the end of the questionnaire.

When to use a questionnaire

A questionnaire can be used to obtain information for:

- sphere of influence
- social surveys
- land uses/land use conflicts
- opinions/preferences
- household surveys.

Top tips

- ✓ Be prepared and well organised.
- ✓ Be polite.
- ✓ Don't ask personal questions.
- ✓ As far as your study allows, try to make sure your questionnaire is representative of the population by ensuring you choose people of all age ranges, genders and ethnicities.

Reasons for using a questionnaire

- A large amount of information can be collected in a short space of time.
- The information collected can usually be processed easily into graphs, charts, etc.
- The Processed Information can be used to compare and contrast.

Example questionnaire

"Hello, I am a student at *Shawlands Academy* and I am conducting a survey about shopping habits as part of my National 5/Higher assignment. Would you mind if I asked you a few quick questions?"

1. Sex   Male ☐   Female ☐

2. Age

   Under 20 ☐   20–30 ☐   30–40 ☐   40–50 ☐   50+ ☐

3. How often do you shop here?

   More than once a week ☐   Every week ☐   Sometimes ☐

4. How far do you travel to visit this shopping centre?

   Within a mile ☐   Within 5 miles ☐   Within 10 miles ☐

5. How do you travel here?

   Car ☐   Bus ☐   Taxi ☐   Other _____

6. Do you ever shop elsewhere?

   Yes ☐   No ☐

   If so, where? _____

"Thank you very much for your time."

Interviews

An interview is simply a way of finding out specific information by asking someone directly.

Equipment required

- ☞ Clipboard
- ☞ Pen/pencil
- ☞ Question sheets

Things to consider ⓘ

Look back at the 'Things to consider' section in Questionnaires for advice on how to create suitable questions for an interview.

When to use an interview

An interview questionnaire can be used to obtain information for:

- sphere of influence
- social surveys
- land uses/land use conflicts

Top tips

✓ Be prepared and well organised.
✓ Be polite.
✓ Don't ask personal questions.
✓ As far as your study allows, try to make sure your interviewees are representative of the population by ensuring you choose people of all age ranges, genders and ethnicities.

- opinions/preferences
- household surveys.

Reasons for using an interview

- A large amount of information can be collected in a short space of time.
- The information collected can usually be processed easily into graphs, charts, etc.
- The Processed Information can be used to compare and contrast.

Activities

1. Working with a partner, choose a topic and then think of some questions to ask your peers in the class.
2. Decide whether you are going to interview your peers or ask them to complete a questionnaire.
3. With your partner, decide:
   a) the style of questions
   b) how many questions to ask
   c) who will write the answers to the questions
   d) who you need to ask, i.e. anyone in the class, or girls/boys only.
4. Carry out your questionnaire/interview.
5. Once you have completed your questionnaire/interview, choose how you would like to present the results, for example, you might choose a bar graph or a pie chart. (For further help in choosing a method to present your results, you might like to refer to Section 2.2 Processing information.)
6. Draw a graph/chart showing the results of your questionnaire/ interview.

Surveys

Undertaking a survey can provide you with lots of useful information for your study. A **land use** survey can be used to assess what the land is being used for in a given area. An **environmental quality** survey can be used to assess the amenities of an area, while a **housing quality** survey and a **shopping quality** survey look at the types and quality of housing and shops respectively in a particular area.

Equipment required

- ☞ Clipboard
- ☞ Pen/pencil
- ☞ Record sheet
- ☞ Camera/camera-phone

Method

This example refers to an environmental quality survey.

1   Before you begin your survey, you must decide on the factors that are relevant to your study. Factors that you might want to consider when conducting an environmental quality survey include:
- nearness to parks
- proximity to schools
- houses with gardens
- amount of woodland/greenery
- amount of litter
- proximity to train lines/stations
- amount of traffic.

2   Next you need to choose your site(s) for conducting the survey. If you are comparing two or more areas, you will need to conduct a survey at each location so that comparisons can be made. You should also think about what time of day you will visit. If you are measuring the amount of traffic, you might want to carry out your survey at peak times of the day, such as 8.30–9.00am or after 5.00pm. Be aware of road safety when carrying out a traffic survey and always put your safety first.

3   There are different ways to record the information you obtain. One option is to set out a table showing the extreme factors on either side, for example, poor environmental quality factors on the left and the good factors on the right, as shown in Table 2.1. An alternative method is to create a table showing the factors in one column, divided into positive and negative factors, as shown in Table 2.2.

4   When at each location, you will need to walk around the area to have a good look. Give each of the factors a score of between 0 and 5, with 0 being the worst and 5 being the best.

5   It is a good idea to take photos to provide evidence for your decisions. You can annotate these photos later to show the reasons for your decisions.

6   Add up the marks to obtain a total score for each site.

Table 2.1 Example of an environmental quality survey

Location 1: Inner-city area						
Lower quality	1	2	3	4	5	Higher quality
No houses have gardens		✓				All houses have gardens
No woodland/greenery in the area		✓				Lots of woodland/greenery in the area
High volume of traffic	✓					Low volume of traffic
Lots of litter	✓					No litter
Total: 6/20						

Things to consider

As this is a method based on personal opinion, the information obtained may not be considered entirely reliable. However, if you choose to back up your decision with photographs it will help to bolster your argument.

Table 2.2 Example of a shopping quality survey

Positive factor	Site 1 (CBD)	Site 2 (Out of town)
Free parking	0	5
Easily accessible	5	3
Variety of shops	5	3
High order shops	4	2
Total: /20	14	13

When to use a survey

A survey can be used to:

- compare settlements/zones in the city
- investigate the functions of settlements.

Reasons for using a survey

- Often the information collected can be processed easily into graphs, charts, etc.
- The Processed Information can be used to compare and contrast.

1 Look at the map extracts below.

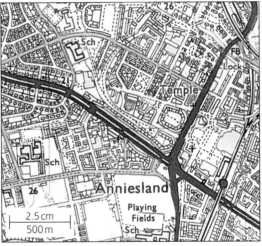

Figure 2.1 Site 1: OS map extract of the Anniesland district of Glasgow

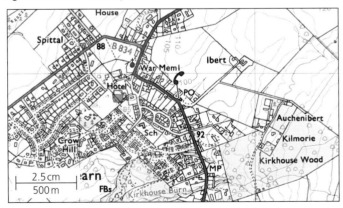

Figure 2.2 Site 2: OS map extract of Killearn, Scotland

Map extracts reproduced by permission © Crown copyright 2017 Ordnance Survey 100047450.

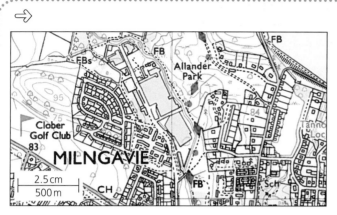

Figure 2.3 Site 3: OS map extract of Milngavie, Scotland

2 Copy and complete the following environmental quality survey for the three sites.

Table 2.3

Factor	Site 1	Site 2	Site 3
Proximity to parks			
Proximity to schools			
Amount of woodland/green spaces			
Access to train/bus stations			
Total: /20			

3 Which site is most pleasant?

Traffic/pedestrian count

A traffic/pedestrian count is used to record the volume of traffic/pedestrians along a particular road.

Equipment required

☞ Clipboard
☞ Pen/pencil
☞ Record sheet

Method

1 Plan your trip beforehand to identify the best location to conduct your count and what time of day would be most relevant to your study. If you are comparing peak morning traffic with mid-afternoon, you will need to do two separate counts.

2 Find a suitable location beside the road with a clear view of the traffic. Make sure you are safe and do not stand right on the kerb.

3 When a car passes you by, put a tally mark on your record sheet.

4 Continue to add tallies every time a car passes.

5 Continue to do this for 10–20 minutes depending on the type of road. If you are recording in a busy, urban area, 10 minutes should be enough, but in a quieter area, 20 minutes might be more appropriate.

6 If you are planning to do another count later on in the day to draw comparisons, you must make sure that you record for the same length of time, so if you record for 10 minutes in the morning, you must record for 10 minutes in the afternoon.

Things to consider

Table 2.4 shows a simple pedestrian count, using tally marks. However, you might want to make your traffic count more specific in terms of the types of vehicles using the roads. Table 2.5 is an example of a table that you could create before you undertake your count.

Table 2.4 Simple pedestrian count

Location: Pollokshaws Road, Glasgow	
Date: 12 November 2016	Time: 08.45–08.55
﹢﹢﹢﹢﹢ ﹢﹢﹢﹢﹢ ‖	

Table 2.5 Detailed traffic count

Location: Pollokshaws Road, Glasgow	
Date: 12 November 2016	Time: 08.45–08.55
Lorries	﹢﹢﹢﹢﹢
Buses	﹢﹢﹢﹢﹢ ﹢﹢﹢﹢﹢ ﹢﹢﹢﹢﹢ ﹢﹢﹢﹢﹢ ﹢﹢﹢﹢﹢
Cars	﹢﹢﹢﹢﹢ ﹢﹢﹢﹢﹢ ﹢﹢﹢﹢﹢ ﹢﹢﹢﹢﹢ ﹢﹢﹢﹢﹢ ﹢﹢﹢﹢﹢ ﹢﹢﹢﹢﹢ ﹢﹢﹢﹢﹢ ﹢﹢﹢﹢﹢
Motorbikes	﹢﹢﹢﹢﹢ ﹢﹢﹢﹢﹢
Vans	﹢﹢﹢﹢﹢ ﹢﹢﹢﹢﹢ ﹢﹢﹢﹢﹢ ﹢﹢﹢﹢﹢

When to use a traffic/pedestrian count

A traffic/pedestrian count can be used to:
- establish the functions of a settlement
- compare inner-city areas
- compare shopping centres.

Reasons for using a traffic/pedestrian count

- The information collected can often be processed easily into graphs, charts, etc.
- The Processed Information can be used to compare and contrast.

Activity

The aim of this count is to compare school corridor activity during the lunch period.

1   Choose two corridors in your school to survey.
2   One person should stand at the entrance to corridor 1 and the other at the entrance to corridor 2.
3   Record every student/teacher/member of staff that passes by in a 10-minute period.
4   Compare your results with your partner.

Land use classification

Land use classification involves analysing and recording land use in a specific area.

Equipment required

☞ Record sheet
☞ Pen/pencil

Method

1   Choose an area and a street within that area where you want to investigate the type of land use.
2   Walk down the street and write down the different types of land use that you find.
3   One of the best ways to classify land use is by using RICE-POTS, which is simply a mnemonic of the different land uses.

Table 2.6

R	Residential
I	Industrial
C	Commercial
E	Entertainment
P	Public buildings
O	Open space
T	Transport
S	Services

4   You could represent the street as a series of rectangles and write down the land use in each individual block or building.

Table 2.7

Main Street looking towards King's Park between Edmonstone Road and Malone Road (right-hand side)									
R	R	C	S	S	R	S	R	R	R
S	C	C	C	C	C	S	C	C	C

5 If you wish to make your classification more specific, you could further classify the land uses to show exactly what types of buildings are located in your chosen street. An example is given below, but you could add more shops/services to this classification system.

Table 2.8

R	Residential	F Flat
		T Terraced house
		S Semi-detached house
		B Bungalow
		D Detached house
I	Industrial	B Building works
		C Chemical
		E Extraction
		H Heavy industry
		L Light industry
C	Commercial	B Beautician
		C Charity shop
		D Department store
		F Food shop
		G Garage
		H Hairdressers
		M Market
		N Newsagent
		O Office
		P Pet shop
		W Warehouse
E	Entertainment	A Arcade
		C Café
		H Hotel
		M Museum
		P Pub
		S Sports centre
		T Theatre/cinema
P	Public buildings	C Church
		E Education/library
		H Hospital/health centre
		J Job centre
		P Police/court
		T Town hall

Table 2.8 (cont.)

O	Open space	A Allotment
		C Cemetery
		D Derelict land
		F Farmland
		S Sports field
		U Unused land
		W Water
T	Transport	A Airport
		B Bus station
		C Car park
		R Railway
		T Taxi rank
S	Services	B Business
		F Financial
		H Housing
		M Medical

6 Using this more detailed classification system, the same example above would become:

Table 2.9

Main Street looking towards King's Park between Edmonstone Road and Malone Road (right-hand side)									
RF	RF	CO	SM	SM	RF	SM	RF	RF	RF
SF	CC	CF	CC	CN	CC	SB	CN	CC	CC

Things to consider

You could colour-code your land use categories to make them even clearer. Remember to include a key too.

When to use a land use map

A land use map can be used for:

- an urban study
- a rural study.

Reasons for using a land use map

- A land use map provides a clear visual representation of the land uses in a particular area.
- It is useful for highlighting specific things, such as how many charity shops are found in an area.

Activities

1 Using the more detailed RICE-POTS classification, what do the following refer to?

   a) RD   d) PC

   b) OF   e) EH

   c) SM   f) IL

2 Using the more simple RICE-POTS classification, record the land uses shown in the image below. Give each land use a specific colour.

Figure 2.4

3 Using the same image, show the more detailed land use classification.

Urban transect

An urban transect involves carrying out fieldwork to determine land use in several places along a line from the CBD (central business district) to the surrounding countryside.

Equipment required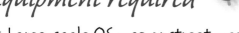

☞ Large-scale OS map or street map
☞ Clipboard
☞ Record sheet
☞ Pen/pencil
☞ Camera/camera-phone

Method

1 Choose a route that you would like to study.
2 Trace a copy of your chosen route onto an OS map or street map.
3 Walk along the route and note down the different land uses on your map. You may wish to use the RICE-POTS land use classification system or you could come up with your own to help you with this.

Things to consider

* If your route shows areas where there are buildings of more than one storey, divide your buildings to show this information.
* You may like to colour your map to show the different land uses – remember to include a key.
* Mapping large areas can be time consuming.

When to use urban transect

Urban transect can be used for:

- land use zones studies
- settlement studies
- population studies.

Reasons for using urban transect

- to show land use patterns
- to highlight specific land uses in an area.

Activities

1 Using an Ordnance Survey map of your local area (1:2500 or 1:250) choose a suitable route for an urban transect.
2 Design your own land use classification system – you can use the RICE-POTS system to help you.
3 Either walk the route or use Google Street View to highlight the land uses along your chosen route.
4 Colour-code your route to show the different land uses and remember to include a key.

Photographs

Photographs are a good way of showing important information. They are also useful to support your argument where information obtained is based on personal opinion.

Equipment required

☞ Camera/camera-phone
☞ Record sheet
☞ Pen/pencil

Method

1 Make sure you are familiar with the camera/camera-phone that you plan to use.
2 Decide the precise view/scene that you want to photograph.

3 If you intend to compare your photograph with another photograph of the same view/scene, make sure that you get the framing right. Try to make sure your photograph includes exactly the same landscape/feature as the other photograph so that direct comparisons can be made.

4 If you take a number of photographs of the same scene, delete the ones you don't need to avoid confusion when you look at the photographs later on.

5 In your record sheet note important information relating to your photograph, such as direction, bearing and details about where it was taken. Remember to give your photograph a title.

> ## *Things to consider*
>
> Poor weather conditions such as mist and fog will prevent you taking a clear photograph so make sure you choose a day when the weather is good.

When to use a photograph

A photograph can be used to illustrate:

- river features/characteristics
- glacial features/characteristics
- coastal landscapes
- limestone landscapes
- farming landscapes
- townscapes.

Reasons for using a photograph

- A photograph can be used for comparison with old/new photographs and for 'before' and 'after' shots.
- It can also be used to identify changes over time.
- Photographs can be annotated to highlight specific features of importance or to look closely at a landscape.

Field sketch

A field sketch is a simple pencil drawing that identifies relevant features of a scene or landscape. An example is shown in Figure 2.5.

Equipment required

☞ Clipboard
☞ Pencil
☞ Rubber
☞ Paper

Method

1 Decide the precise area that you are going to sketch.

2 If you intend to compare your sketch to an old or new photograph for example, make sure that you get the framing right. Try to make sure your sketch includes exactly the same landscape/feature as the photograph so that direct comparisons can be made.

3 Depending on what you are sketching, it might be helpful to divide your paper into thirds, showing the foreground, middle ground and background.

4 You should start by sketching the things in the background and work forwards.

5 Add only the detail that is important to your study.

6 You could use shading or colour to highlight specific features of importance.

7 Label your sketch with a heading, direction, bearing and details about where it was drawn. You might also want to annotate it with specific features at this point.

Things to consider

If the weather is poor, you could take a photograph of the scene and use it to draw a field sketch at home or in school.

When to use a field sketch

A field sketch can be used to illustrate:

- river features/characteristics
- glacial features/characteristics
- coastal landscapes
- limestone landscapes
- farming landscapes.

Reasons for using a field sketch

- A field sketch can be used for comparison with old/new photographs.
- You can use colour and annotate a field sketch in order to highlight specific features of importance.
- A field sketch enables you to look closely at a landscape.

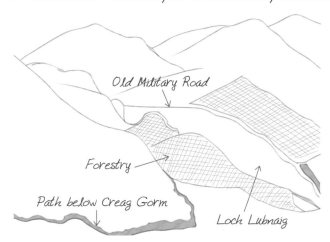

Figure 2.5 Field sketch

1 Look at the photograph of the Dorset Coast below.

Figure 2.6

2 Using this photograph, draw a field sketch of this area.
3 Annotate your sketch with key information.

Measuring soil moisture content

The soil moisture content is simply the amount of water contained in a soil sample.

Equipment required

☞ Trowel or spade
☞ Zip-seal bags
☞ Plastic containers
☞ Weighing scales
☞ Pen/pencil
☞ Record sheet

Method

1 In the field, use a trowel or spade to take a small sample of topsoil from your chosen site.
2 Place this sample into a zip-seal bag.
3 On returning from the field, take each sample and put it into a separate pre-weighed empty plastic container.
4 Weigh the soil in the plastic container and mark it on your record sheet.
5 Leave the soil sample for a week to allow any moisture to evaporate.
6 Weigh each container again.

7   Mark the new weight on your record sheet.
8   Subtract the weight of the empty plastic container.
9   Subtract the dry soil weight from the original weight to find how much moisture was in the soil at each site.

> ### Things to consider ❗
>
> Depending on your study you might decide to measure soil moisture at a particular time, for example, after a period of heavy rainfall.
>
> Conduct your study at a time to suit you.
>
> It is important to remain safe when carrying out fieldwork.

When to measure soil moisture content

Measuring soil moisture content can be used:
- as part of a river study
- to determine the factors affecting soil moisture.

Reason for measuring soil moisture content

The information collected can be used to compare with other samples.

Vegetation transect

A vegetation transect is a line across a habitat where a number of species or plant communities can be observed and recorded at regular intervals.

Equipment required

☞ Metre stick/ruler
☞ 20m measuring tape
☞ Camera/camera-phone
☞ Record sheet
☞ Pen/pencil
☞ Plant guide

Method

1   Select an area where you want to carry out your line transect.
2   Secure the measuring tape at the start location and extend the tape in the direction of your line transect for 20m until you reach the end point. Secure the tape in place.
3   Starting at the beginning, walk along the tape. For every plant that touches the line, record where it is (distance from the start) and the height of the plant.
4   If you are unsure what a particular plant is, take a photograph of it so that you can look it up later.

Things to consider

Vegetation transects cannot tell you the density of plant communities in an area.

When to carry out a vegetation transect

A vegetation transect can be carried out as part of a:
- coastal study – to identify vegetation along sand dunes
- glacial study – looking at vegetation found in upland glaciated areas
- limestone study – to identify vegetation found on a limestone pavement
- river study – to identify vegetation found along a riverbank.

Reasons for using a vegetation transect

The information collected can be displayed clearly in a kite diagram. Kite diagrams can be used to compare different sites.

Activities

1 Choose a location within your school grounds to carry out a transect. For example, you could choose the playing fields, the school garden or even along the edges of the playground.
2 Carry out a vegetation transect of this area.
3 Record this information in your notebook.
4 Draw a kite diagram to show your findings.

Measuring slope angle

Slope angle is a measurement to work out how steep or gentle a slope is. A clinometer can be used to measure slope angle, but if you do not have one, then you can make one using a protractor, some string and a weight.

Equipment required

☞ Record sheet
☞ Pen/pencil
☞ Protractor
☞ String
☞ Weight

Method

To make a clinometer using a protractor:
1 Attach the string to the protractor at the 'centre point'.
2 Attach the weight to the piece of string. The weight can be anything – a pencil, magnet, rubber or bolt.

3   The weight should hang down over 0° when the straight edge of the protractor is parallel to the ground (see Figure 2.7).

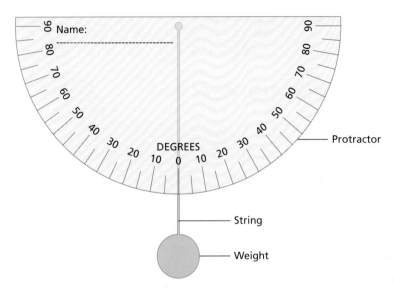

Figure 2.7 How to make a clinometer using a protractor

To measure slope angle:

1   You can either measure slope angle from the top of the hill or the bottom.
2   From the bottom of the hill, look uphill along the straight edge of the protractor.
3   The string will hang over the angle of the slope (see Figure 2.8).
4   Check this angle and write it down.
5   Alternatively, if you have a clinometer, you can use that to find out the slope angle.

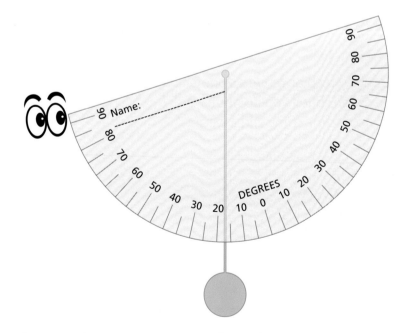

Figure 2.8 Using a protractor to measure slope angle

Activity

Using the information in this section make your own clinometer.

When to measure slope angle

Measuring slope angle can be used in a:

- glacial study – to measure the slope angle of drumlins
- river study – to compare the slope angle in upper and lower courses
- coastal study – measuring the slope angle of dunes.

Measuring height

You may need to measure the height of a slope or cliff as part of your investigation.

Equipment required

☞ Record sheet
☞ Pen/pencil
☞ Tape measure
☞ Clinometer (see 'Measuring slope angle' for information on making your own clinometer)
☞ Calculator

Method

1 Measure the distance from where you are standing or from your marker to the base of the cliff (distance A – see Figure 2.9). Record this measurement on your record sheet.
2 Using your clinometer and with your eye at 0°, swivel the clinometer until it points towards the top of the cliff (distance B). Write down the measurement on your record sheet.
3 To find the height of the cliff, use the following calculation:
Height of cliff = distance (A) × tan of angle (B) + height of clinometer from ground
4 Here is a worked example:
A = 10 m
Slope = 65°
Height of clinometer from ground = 1.67 m
Height of cliff = 10 × tan 65 + 1.67 = 23.1 m

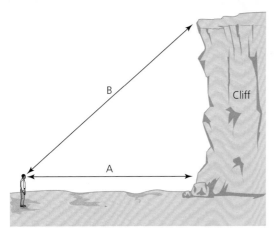

Figure 2.9 Measuring the height of a cliff

 Things to consider (!)

To make your clinometer as accurate as possible, you could stand a 1.5 metre pole at the top and bottom of the slope and look upwards from that height.

When to measure height

Measuring height can be useful when undertaking:
- a coastal/glacial study – to measure the height of steep cliffs
- an urban study – to measure the height of buildings.

 Activities

1 Work out the following heights:
   a) Olivia is 1.56 metres tall and she stood 15 metres from the base of the cliff. Using her clinometer, she measured the angle of the slope to be 76°. What is the height of this cliff?
   b) Ross is working out the height of some of the tallest buildings in Glasgow. He is 1.65 metres tall and he stood a distance of 5 metres from the bottom of the tallest building. The angle of the slope is 90°. What is the height of the tallest building?
2 Using the clinometer you made in 'Measuring slope angle', measure the height of some of the buildings in your school.

Measuring stone size and shape

The rocks, stones and sand carried by a river are referred to as its 'load'. Measuring stone size and shape can help you determine the bed load of a river or measure deposits on a beach.

Equipment required

☞ Clipboard
☞ Record sheet
☞ Pen/pencil
☞ Ruler
☞ Measuring tape

Method

Size

1 Reach down into the river and pick up the first stone that your hand meets.
2 Record the distance from the bank that you found this stone.
3 Measure the longest axis of this stone (axis A – see Figure 2.10 on page 30).
4 Record your findings.
5 Repeat this ten times per location.

Shape

A roundness index (Table 2.10) is used to work out the shape of the stones. The information in Table 2.10 can also be used to work out the shape of the load of a river, as shown in Table 2.11.

Table 2.10 Roundness index of stones

Class 1	Class 2	Class 3	Class 4	Class 5	Class 6
Very angular	Angular	Sub-angular	Sub-rounded	Rounded	Well-rounded

Table 2.11 Working out the shape of the load of a river

Distance from the bank (m)	0	0.2	0.4	0.6	0.8	1.0	1.2
A axis (cm)	11.2	9.8	9.2	6.3	8.8	7.9	10.3
B axis (cm)	9.8	8.6	8.3	5.4	7.9	7.1	9.7
C axis (cm)	8.4	7.6	7.9	4.8	6.9	6.4	8.4
Shape	Sub-angular	Sub-angular	Sub-rounded	Sub-angular	Sub-rounded	Sub-rounded	Sub-rounded

Things to consider

Depending on your study you may want to work out the A, B and C axes for each of the stones in your sample.

A = long axis

B = middle axis

C = short axis

Figure 2.10 shows the A, B and C axes of a stone. You can use your ruler to measure each axis.

The method described above will only work out the bed load of the river; it will not tell you the suspended load or dissolved load.

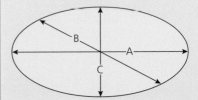

Figure 2.10 A, B and C axes of a stone

When to measure stone shape and size

Measuring stone shape and size can be used during a:

- river study – to measure the load of the river
- coastal study – to measure beach deposits
- glacial study – to measure the till/scree deposits.

Activity

1 Select ten stones from the school playground.
2 Record their size and shape using the information above.
3 Compare your results with a partner.

Using the internet

The internet is a great tool for researching information of all kinds, but always make sure you are careful about what websites you look at and how you enter things into a search engine. Here are some websites which you may find helpful while undertaking your research:

www.sns.gov.uk – Scottish Neighbourhood Statistics

www.scotlandscensus.gov.uk or www.scrol.gov.uk – Scotland's census

www.ons.gov.uk – Office for National Statistics

www.streetcheck.co.uk – provides lots of statistical information on your local area

www.who.int/whosis – WHO Statistical Information System

2.2
Processing information

Bar graph

A bar graph can be used to:
- compare different information
- show trends
- highlight changes over time.

Advantages of using this technique
- Comparisons can be made between data easily.
- Relationships between data can be identified quickly.
- Bar graphs are effective in showing trends or changes over a period of time.

Examples

There are three types of bar graph:
- vertical
- horizontal
- stacked.

Vertical bar graph

This is arguably the most common type of bar graph used. The data can be easily read and interpreted and comparisons can be made easily. In a vertical bar graph the labels are shown along the x axis.

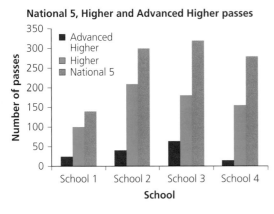

Figure 2.11 Bar graph

Figure 2.11 shows the number of students in four different schools that achieved National 5, Higher and Advanced Higher certificates. Showing the information in this way allows us to clearly see which school had the most passes at the different levels.

Horizontal bar graph

A horizontal bar graph can be used to show the same information as a vertical bar graph, but the main difference is that the labels are shown along the y axis (Figure 2.12). If your labels are very long, you might prefer to use a horizontal bar graph.

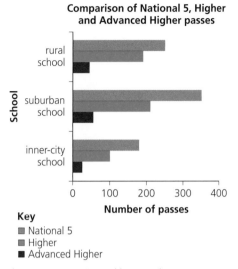

Figure 2.12 Horizontal bar graph

Stacked bar graph

A stacked bar graph is used when there are so many sets of data to show that it would be impractical to use a vertical or horizontal bar graph.

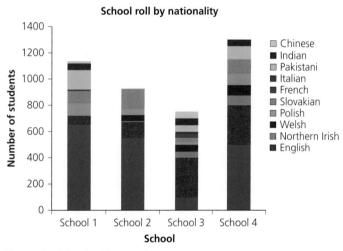

Figure 2.13 Stacked bar graph

The main drawback to using this type of graph is that it can be very difficult to interpret, particularly if there are many sets of data.

Stacked bar graphs should not be confused with divided bar graphs, which will be explained later in this section.

Things to consider (!)

When drawing any type of bar graph, there are a number of things you should bear in mind:

* Always give your graph a title; this allows the reader to understand what the graph shows.
* Similarly, both the x and y axes should be given titles.

* Use a suitable scale. Your graph should always start at 0 and must go up to your highest number.
* Choose an appropriate range to go up in. Depending on the data used, it is usually easiest to go up in 5s, 10s, 50s, 100s, etc.
* Each bar should be the same width and the gaps between columns should be the same distance apart.
* Colour each bar a different colour as this makes it easier for comparisons to be made.
* Include a key, if necessary.
* If you are using more than one bar graph to make comparisons, make sure you use the same range for each graph, otherwise your findings will look distorted.
* Similarly, if you are using different colours for each bar, make sure you use the same colours on the comparison graph.

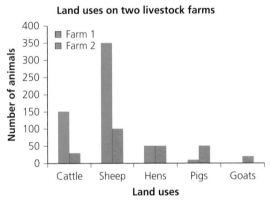

Figure 2.14 Bar graph showing the land uses on two different livestock farms

Activities

1 The information in the table below shows the ten worst natural disasters by death toll. Draw either a vertical or horizontal bar graph to show the information.

Table 2.12

Natural disaster	Death toll
China floods	1,000,000+
Yellow River flood, China	900,000
Shaanxi earthquake, China	830,000
Tanshan earthquake, China	450,000
Bhola cyclone, Bangladesh	375,000
India cyclone	300,000
Calcutta cyclone	300,000
Indian Ocean earthquake and tsunami	280,000
Haiyuan earthquake, China	273,000
Antioch earthquake, Turkey	250,000

2 Three shop owners asked 500 customers which area they lived in. The results are shown below. Draw a stacked bar graph to show this information.

Table 2.13

Fruit	Shop 1	Shop 2	Shop 3
Shawlands	120	80	250
Battlefield	80	65	90
Govanhill	30	85	0
Gorbals	15	110	10
Govan	25	150	5
Newlands	115	5	100
Muirend	65	5	25
Cathcart	50	0	20

Top tips

Remember to:

✓ give your graph a title
✓ choose a suitable scale for the *y* axis
✓ give both *x* and *y* axes a title
✓ make sure each bar is the same width apart
✓ colour each bar a different colour
✓ include a key if necessary.

Dot plot graph

A dot plot graph can be used to:

● show comparisons
● show frequencies.

Advantages of using this technique

● A dot plot graph enables comparisons between the data to be made quickly.
● This type of graph is very simple and easy to understand.

Example

A dot plot graph can be used for small sets of data. It is similar to a bar graph and is often used as an alternative.

First, each dot is given a value (usually one). The dots are then stacked on top of each other to show how many belong to each category. For example, Figure 2.15 shows how long it takes a group of students to walk home from school. Each dot represents one student.

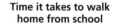

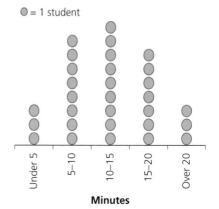

Figure 2.15 Dot plot graph

Things to consider

* A dot plot graph is most appropriate for smaller data sets.
* Each dot should be made the same size; larger or smaller dots may be misinterpreted as having a higher or lower value.
* Keep the graph simple. The main advantage of a dot plot graph is its simplicity, which makes it so easy to interpret.
* It is preferable to retain the same colour for each dot in the graph; using multiple colours can make the graph confusing to interpret.
* A dot plot graph can really only be used with whole numbers. It is possible to round data up or down to the nearest whole number, but inevitably this makes the graph less accurate.

Activity

1   A class of 30 students studying Geography in S2 was asked what topics they would like to study. The results are shown below.

Table 2.14

Topic	Number of students
Earthquakes and volcanoes	19
Natural wonders	8
Global warming	3

2   Draw a dot plot graph to show this information.
3   What is wrong with the results?

Pictograph

A pictograph (also known as a pictogram) is used in a similar way to a bar graph. It is used to:
* show trends in data
* compare information.

Advantages of using this technique

* A pictograph is generally easy to read.
* It is a fun way of showing information.

Example

A pictograph uses pictures or symbols to represent data. There are two main ways of presenting information on a pictograph. Figure 2.16 shows a group of students' favourite fruit, represented by symbols of each type of fruit. An alternative way to show information that is very similar to a bar graph is depicted in Figure 2.17, detailing the length of five of the longest rivers in Scotland. Instead of the data being drawn as bars, it is shown as blue curvy lines, to represent a river.

Students' favourite fruit

Figure 2.16 Pictograph using symbols

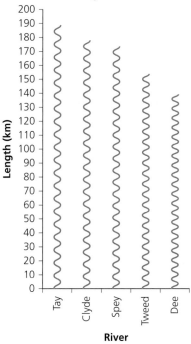

Figure 2.17 Pictograph in the form of a bar graph

Things to consider

* Remember to give your graph a title.
* Make sure that your data is easily transferable to a pictograph as not all data lends itself to this form of representation.
* Pictographs are not the most accurate way of showing information. If your data is not in whole numbers or has small values it will be difficult to represent accurately.
* Always take care when drawing your pictograph so that the information shown is accurate.
* Not all pictographs require a key, but if yours does make sure you include one.

Activity

The information in the table shows the populations of the four countries of the United Kingdom in 2013/14. Draw a pictograph to show this information.

Table 2.15

Country	Population (millions)
Scotland	5.3
Northern Ireland	1.8
Wales	3.0
England	54.3

Top tips

Remember to:
✓ choose a suitable picture/symbol for your pictograph
✓ give your pictograph a title
✓ choose a suitable scale for the y axis
✓ give both the x and y axes a title
✓ include a key if necessary.

Line graph

A line graph is used in a similar way to a bar graph. It can:
- track changes over periods of time
- show trends and patterns
- show relationships between data
- be used to make comparisons and trends.

Advantages of using this technique

- A line graph is generally easy to read.
- It provides an effective way of showing patterns and relationships in data.
- A line graph is easy to interpret.

Types of line graph

There are two types of line graph:
- single
- multiple.

Single line graph

One of the most common uses of a line graph is to show changes over a period of time. In Geography, temperature is often shown using a line graph.

Figure 2.18 is a line graph which shows changes in average temperature in Glasgow over a period of one year. From the graph it is very easy to see how the temperature fluctuates throughout the year. This information is immediately visible. The graph is easily interpreted and shows the information effectively. One of the main benefits of using a line graph is that it allows each change to be seen and an overall pattern to be identified.

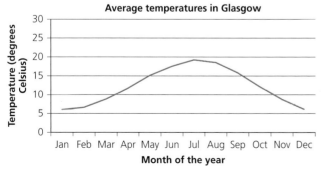

Figure 2.18 Single line graph

Multiple line graph

A single line graph is used when there is only one variable to be shown. A multiple line graph is used when there are several variables. This may be to show changes over large periods of time such as months or years. The graph in Figure 2.19 shows the average temperatures in Scotland in 2015, compared to the previous three years. In order to make this graph as easy to interpret as possible, it is helpful to use a different colour for each year. If you are plotting points, you may also want to use different shapes for each variable.

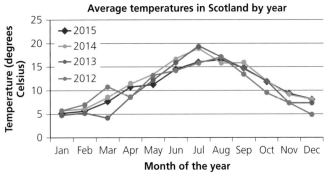

Figure 2.19 Multiple line graph

Things to consider

* Always give your graph a title; this allows the reader to understand what the graph shows.
* Similarly, both the *x* and *y* axes should be given titles.
* Use a suitable scale. Your graph should always start at 0 and must go up to your highest number.
* Choose an appropriate range to go up in. Depending on the data used, it is usually easiest to go up in 5s, 10s, 50s, 100s, etc.
* Include a key, if necessary.
* If you are using a multiple line graph to make comparisons, make sure you clearly differentiate between each line – using colour is a good way to do this.

Activities

1 Table 2.16 below shows how the population of the UK has changed since the year 2000. Draw a single line graph to show this information.

Table 2.16

Year	Population (millions)
2000	59.0
2001	59.1
2002	59.4
2003	59.6
2004	60.0
2005	60.4
2006	60.8
2007	61.3

Table 2.16 (cont.)

Year	Population (millions)
2008	61.8
2009	62.2
2010	62.7
2011	63.3
2012	63.7
2013	64.1
2014	64.6

⇨

2 Table 2.17 below shows how the population of each of the four countries in the UK has changed since the year 2000. Draw a multiple line graph to show this information.

Table 2.17

Year	Scotland population (millions)	Northern Ireland population (millions)	Wales population (millions)	England population (millions)
2000	5.1	1.6	2.9	49.2
2001	5.1	1.6	2.9	49.9
2002	5.1	1.7	2.9	50.2
2003	5.1	1.7	2.9	50.6
2004	5.1	1.7	2.9	50.9
2005	5.1	1.7	2.9	51.2
2006	5.1	1.7	2.9	51.5
2007	5.1	1.7	2.9	51.8
2008	5.1	1.8	2.9	52.0
2009	5.2	1.8	2.9	52.4
2010	5.2	1.8	3.0	52.7
2011	5.3	1.8	3.0	53.0
2012	5.3	1.8	3.0	53.7
2013	5.3	1.8	3.0	54.1
2014	5.3	1.8	3.0	54.3

Top tips

Remember to:

✓ give your graph a title
✓ choose a suitable scale for the y axis
✓ give both the x and y axes a title
✓ make sure that each year along the x axis is the same distance apart
✓ include a key if necessary.

Scatter graph

A scatter graph is used to:
- determine if there is a relationship between two variables (factors) – which may be positive or negative
- show trends over time
- make predictions.

Advantages of using this technique

- A scatter graph is usually easy to read.
- It is an effective way of showing patterns and relationships in data.
- A scatter graph is easy to interpret.

Example

Table 2.18 shows two variables – the speed of a river and the depth. The aim of the study is to determine if there is a relationship between the speed and depth.

Figure 2.20 shows how the findings in Table 2.18 would look on a scatter graph.

Table 2.18 Speed and depth of a river

Depth (metres)	0.2	0.4	0.6	0.8	1.0	1.2	1.4	1.6	1.8	2.0
Speed (seconds)	32	29	25	23	20	17	14	12	9	6

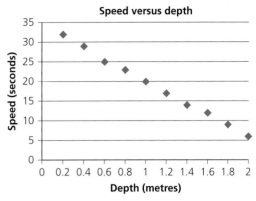

Figure 2.20 Scatter graph

Looking at Figure 2.20, it is very clear that there is a relationship between the speed of the river and its depth – the deeper the river, the slower the speed. When the scatter graph descends as in Figure 2.20, there is a negative correlation. If the graph ascends, there is a positive correlation.

The 'line of best fit' shows how strong the correlation is. This is a line drawn approximately through the middle of the scatter graph points, as shown in Figure 2.21. The closer all the points are to the line, the stronger the correlation. In Figure 2.21 there is a strong correlation between the speed of the river and the depth.

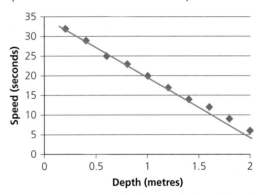

Figure 2.21 Scatter graph showing the line of best fit

Things to consider

* Always give your graph a title; this allows the reader to understand what the graph shows.
* Similarly, both the *x* and *y* axes should be given titles.
* The dependent (response) variable should be shown on the vertical axis (*y* axis) and the independent (explanatory) variable should be on the horizontal axis (*x* axis).
* Use a suitable scale. Your graph should always start at 0 and must go up to your highest number.
* Choose an appropriate range to go up in. Depending on the data used, it is usually easiest to go up in 5s, 10s, 50s, 100s, etc.
* Include a key, if necessary.
* The best way of identifying whether there is a connection between two variables is to use Spearman's rank correlation coefficient (see later in this section).

Activity

As part of a high school study, 20 people were asked their age and the time it takes them to get ready for school in the morning (to the nearest 10 minutes). The average results for each year group are shown in the table.

Draw a scatter graph to show this information.

Table 2.19

Age	Time (minutes)
11	30
12	40
13	60
14	60
15	80
16	90
17	90
18	100

Pie chart and divided bar graph

A pie chart and a divided bar graph are both used to show:

- percentages
- how a 'whole' is divided into parts.

Advantages of using these techniques

- Pie charts and divided bar graphs are visually appealing.
- Both are easy to interpret as each segment of the pie or bar can be a different colour to make comparison easy.

Examples

Pie chart

A pie chart is a good method of showing information that is represented by percentages.

The full circle represents one whole or 100 per cent and each segment represents a particular share of that whole.

If the information is already shown in percentages, then drawing a pie chart is reasonably straightforward. Table 2.20 shows the land uses on a farm, while Figure 2.22 shows the same information as a pie chart.

Table 2.20 Land uses on a farm

Land use	Sheep	Cattle	Poultry	Fodder crops
Percentage	45	25	15	15

Land uses on a farm

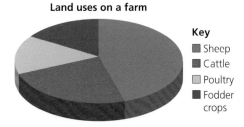

Key
- Sheep
- Cattle
- Poultry
- Fodder crops

Figure 2.22 Pie chart showing land uses on a farm

If the information is not in percentages and you want to show it as such, you will need to convert the information into a percentage for each segment. For example, Table 2.21 shows the age categories of students on a school trip.

Table 2.21 Age categories of students on a school trip

Age category	Number of students	% of students
13	80	40
14	77	38.5
15	24	12
16	19	9.5

To work out the percentage of students of each age category on the school trip, divide the number of students in each age group by the total number of students then multiply the answer by 100. For example:

Number of students/Total number of students × 100 = Percentage of students of each age category on trip

Example

$\frac{80}{200} = 0.4 \times 100 = 40\%$ of students aged 13 on school trip

Figure 2.23 shows how the information would appear on a pie chart.

To make it clear exactly what percentage is allocated to each segment, it is helpful to annotate each segment of your pie chart with the actual figures, as shown in Figure 2.23.

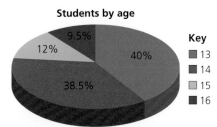

Figure 2.23 Pie chart showing percentage of students on a school trip by age

Today, pie charts tend to be produced using a computer program. However, if you don't have access to a computer or would prefer to draw your pie chart by hand, here is how you work out the angles of each segment:

$$\frac{\text{Number of students}}{\text{Total number of students}} \times 360 = \text{Angle of segment}$$

Example

$\frac{80}{200} = 0.4 \times 360 = 144°$ (segment for students aged 13 on school trip)

Divided bar graph

A divided bar graph is similar to a pie chart as it also shows how a 'whole' is divided into parts. Instead of the information being shown in a circular model it is shown as a rectangle or bar. It is then divided into parts which show how much each category is worth.

For example, the information shown in the pie chart in Figure 2.22 can also be shown as a divided bar graph, as in Figure 2.24.

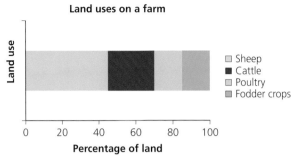

Figure 2.24 Divided bar graph

Again, to make the data clearer and to save the interpreter from having to work things out, you could annotate your divided bar graph with the actual percentages (Figure 2.25).

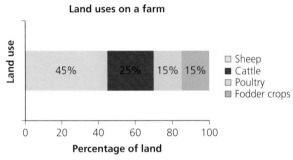

Figure 2.25 Annotated divided bar graph

Things to consider

* Make sure your chart/graph is visually appealing. One of the best ways to do this is by colouring each segment a different colour.
* Colouring each segment a different colour makes it easy to compare.

Activity

100 Geography students were asked what Geography topics they enjoyed learning the most. The results are shown below.

Table 2.22

Geography topic	Number of students
Rivers	20
Limestone	5
Population	10
Urban	5
Earthquakes & volcanoes	60

Show this information in either a pie chart or a divided bar graph.

Kite diagram

A kite diagram is used to show the distribution of organisms along a transect.

Advantages of using this technique

- A kite diagram highlights changes over a specific distance.
- This type of diagram is clear and easy to interpret.
- A kite diagram enables comparisons to be made.

Example

After completing a vegetation transect, you can use the results to draw a kite diagram. You will need to draw a kite diagram for every plant species you identified. Table 2.23 shows the information collected from a vegetation transect.

Table 2.23 Information collected from a vegetation transect

Distance (m)	Daisies	Dandelions	Grasses
0.0	2	0	0
1.0	3	0	1
2.0	4	0	2
3.0	5	1	3
4.0	3	2	2
5.0	1	3	1
6.0	0	2	1
7.0	0	1	2
8.0	0	0	3
9.0	0	0	2
10.0	0	0	1

Figure 2.26 shows this same information on a kite diagram.

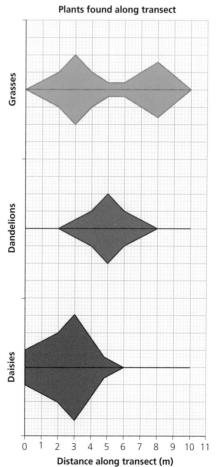

Plants found along transect

Grasses

Dandelions

Daisies

Distance along transect (m)

Figure 2.26 Kite diagram

In Figure 2.26 the x axis shows the distance along the transect and the y axis shows the different plant species that were identified and the number found. To plot the points, draw a line through the middle of each species, half your results and plot the points above and below the mid-line. Join the dots and colour each 'kite'.

Things to consider

* Always give your graph a title; this allows the reader to understand what the graph shows.
* Similarly, both the x and y axes should be given titles.
* To choose a scale, you need to work out what your highest range is.
* Include a key, if necessary.

Activity

1 Using the information in the table below, draw your own kite diagrams.
2 Colour each 'kite' a different colour.
3 Describe the distribution of plants found along this transect.

Table 2.24

Distance (m)	Sea rocket	Marram grass	Heather
0.0	1	0	0
2.0	4	0	0
4.0	6	0	0
6.0	3	3	0
8.0	0	6	0
10.0	0	8	3
12.0	0	5	4
14.0	0	2	6
16.0	0	0	8

Tabulating information

Data that is displayed in a table (tabulated) can be used to:
● compare
● highlight changes
● organise findings.

Advantages of using this technique

● A table is easy to interpret.
● Tabulated information is clear and enables comparisons to be made between variables.

Example

Choosing to show your data in a table rather than a graph is perfectly acceptable. A table is a good method of showing information in a clear, visual way. Sometimes plotting data in a graph is not the best way to display it and keeping it simple may be a better choice.

There are many reasons why a table is used to show data. It can show patterns or help to make comparisons. In fieldwork, data is often both recorded in and presented in a table.

A group of students are conducting a river study. The aim of their study is to find out if the size of the load changes downstream. In order to investigate this, the students must collect a sample of ten stones from three different sites downstream. The most efficient way of recording this information is to use a table. The students' findings are shown in Table 2.25.

Table 2.25 Stone samples collected from three sites on a river

Site 1										
Stone	1	2	3	4	5	6	7	8	9	10	Average
Size	35	38	52	27	36	24	19	28	23	39	32
Site 2										
Stone	1	2	3	4	5	6	7	8	9	10	Average
Size	22	19	28	16	14	18	29	24	31	22	22
Site 3										
Stone	1	2	3	4	5	6	7	8	9	10	Average
Size	9	3	11	8	11	6	14	2	6	9	8

Although the information in Table 2.25 is clear, you might decide to take the information you need and further tabulate it to make it simpler to interpret and make comparisons easier. Table 2.26 shows this data further condensed.

Table 2.26 Average size of samples collected from three sites on a river

Site	1	2	3
Average size (cm)	32	22	8

Things to consider

Not all data lends itself to tabulation; some data is better presented as a graph.

Activity

A student has collected the following information after completing a river study.

Upper course

The river's speed was measured at five different points in the upper course. At site 1, the speed was 23 m/s, at site 2 the speed was 27 m/s, at site 3 the speed was 24 m/s, at site 4 the speed was 23 m/s and at site 5 the speed was 26 m/s.

Middle course

The river's speed was measured at five different points in the middle course. At site 1, the speed was 26 m/s, at site 2 the speed was 28 m/s, at site 3 the speed was 30 m/s, at site 4 the speed was 27 m/s and at site 5 the speed was 31 m/s.   ⇨

Lower course

The river's speed was measured at five different points in the lower course. At site 1, the speed was 35 m/s, at site 2 the speed was 36 m/s, at site 3 the speed was 34 m/s, at site 4 the speed was 35m/s and at site 5 the speed was 36 m/s.

1 Sort the information given above into table form. You may draw three tables or include all the information in one table.
2 Now put the information into a multiple line graph.
3 Which method of presenting this information (table or graph) do you think is clearer? Why?

Cross-section using an OS map

Equipment required

☞ OS map
☞ Plain paper
☞ Pencil
☞ Ruler

Method

1 Using your OS map, find the 6-figure grid reference point where you want to start and end your cross-section (Figure 2.27a).
2 Place a piece of plain paper along the map connecting these two points (Figure 2.27b).
3 Mark on the paper the 6-figure grid reference points as a line (Figure 2.27b).
4 Mark a point where each 'darker' 50 metre contour line crosses the edge of the paper from your beginning point to the end (Figure 2.27b).
5 The darker contour lines have heights attached to them. Find out the height of the land for each line and mark this on your paper (Figure 2.27b).
6 Mark on any specific feature, such as rivers, roads, etc.
7 Take another piece of paper and line your 'marked' sheet along the base of the paper (this will now be your x axis).
8 Your y axis will show the height of the land and will most likely go up in 50s.
9 For every contour line shown on your paper find the height on the y axis and mark a point. Do this for every darker contour line (Figure 2.27c).
10 When you've finished you will have marked in all the contour lines (Figure 2.27d).
11 Join all of the dots together to show the cross-sectional profile of the area in question (Figure 2.28).

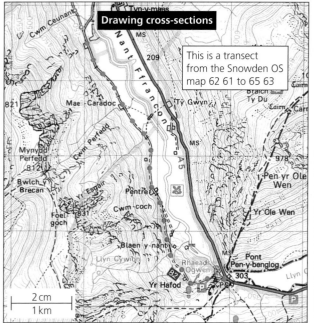

Drawing cross-sections

This is a transect from the Snowden OS map 62 61 to 65 63

Figure 2.27a

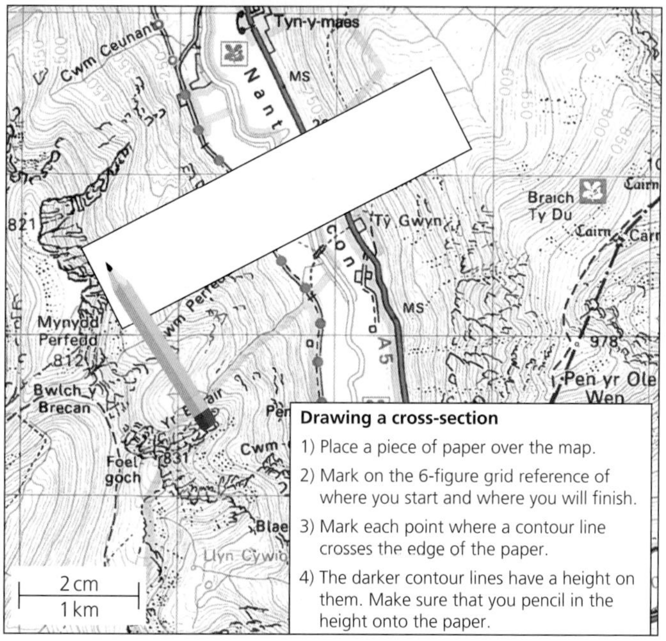

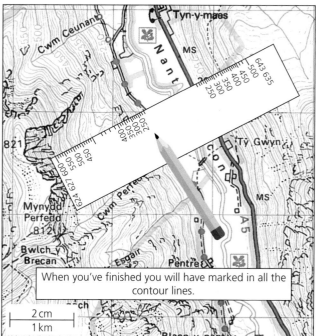

Drawing a cross-section

1) Place a piece of paper over the map.

2) Mark on the 6-figure grid reference of where you start and where you will finish.

3) Mark each point where a contour line crosses the edge of the paper.

4) The darker contour lines have a height on them. Make sure that you pencil in the height onto the paper.

Figure 2.27b

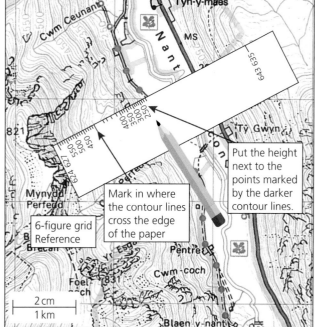

Put the height next to the points marked by the darker contour lines.

Mark in where the contour lines cross the edge of the paper

6-figure grid Reference

Figure 2.27c

When you've finished you will have marked in all the contour lines.

Figure 2.27d

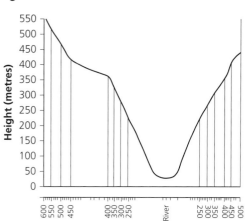

Figure 2.28

Map extracts reproduced by permission © Crown copyright 2017 Ordnance Survey 100047450.

Activity

Using the map extract shown below, draw a cross-section of the area between 380175 and 405175.

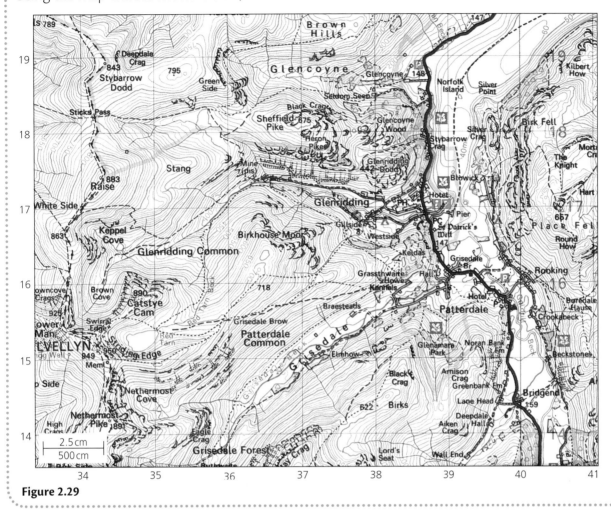

Figure 2.29

How to draw a slope profile

Equipment required

☞ Information collected in the field for angle of slope and
   distance between clinometer and top of the slope.
☞ Protractor
☞ Compass
☞ Pencil
☞ Ruler
☞ Paper
☞ Rubber

Method

1 Choose a suitable scale to show the distance from the clinometer to
   the top of the slope, for example, 1 cm = 10 m.
2 Draw a straight line along the base of a piece of paper and mark where
   the clinometer was located at one end of the line.

3 Place the protractor at the end of the line where the clinometer was placed and draw a line in the direction of the slope angle. For example, if your slope was 65°, use the protractor to measure a line from the 65° mark.

4 Using a compass, open it out to the distance of your slope. For example, if your slope was 50 m and you are using a scale of 1 cm = 10 m you should open your compass 5 cm.

5 With the needle point at the location of the clinometer, draw an arc. Where the arc overlaps the straight line, this marks the point where your slope ends.

6 Draw a line from that point to the line at the base (to form a triangle).

7 Rub out any unwanted pencil marks.

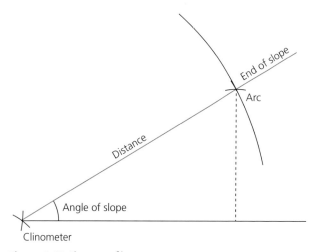

Figure 2.30 Slope profile

Activity

Draw the slope profile for the slopes shown in the table.

Table 2.27

	Angle of slope	Length of slope (m)
A	65°	15
B	40°	22
C	55°	20
D	70°	25
E	35°	20

2.3
Useful calculations

Mean, mode, median, inter-quartile range and standard deviation

Mean is another word for 'average'.

Mode is the name given to a number that appears most often in a set of data.

Median is the middle number.

Inter-quartile range is a way of measuring how spread out the data is.

Standard deviation is how much values have deviated from the average.

Examples

Mean

The mean is the total of a set of values divided by how many values there are.

For example, the average monthly temperatures in one year are as follows:

J	F	M	A	M	J	J	A	S	O	N	D
7	11	12	16	16	18	21	19	15	12	9	5

To find out the 'mean' temperature you would add all the monthly temperatures together:

7 + 11 + 12 + 16 + 16 + 18 + 21 + 19 + 15 + 12 + 9 + 5 = 161

Divide the total by the number of months:

$$\frac{161}{12} = 13$$

Therefore, the mean temperature is 13°.

Mode

The mode is the number that occurs most frequently in a set of values. The mode does not always have to have a numerical value; it can be used for any type of data. For example, a study along a river course showed there were:

- 3 waterfalls
- 27 meanders
- 19 river cliffs
- 19 river beaches
- 1 oxbow lake.

The mode in this example is meander, as there were more of these than any other feature.

A numerical example would be to find the mode of the number of hours a shop is open each week.

Table 2.28

Day	Hours
Mon	8
Tue	8
Wed	8
Thu	11
Fri	8
Sat	9
Sun	9

The mode here is 8. On four days the shop is open for 8 hours, on two days it is open for 9 hours and on one day the shop is open for 11 hours.

Median

The median is the middle number in a list or sequence of numbers. In order to work out the median, you must first sort the numbers into chronological order. For example:

Table 2.29

	Speed of a river				
Attempt	1	2	3	4	5
Seconds	18	16	19	18	20

The sequence is: 18, 16, 19, 18, 20

Sorting them into order becomes: 16, 18, 18, 19, 20

The middle number is: 18

If you have an even number of values, you need to calculate the mean of the two middle numbers. For example:

Sequence: 13, 9, 16, 7, 15, 18

In order: 7, 9, 13, 15, 16, 18

13 and 15 are the middle numbers therefore the median is:

$13 + 15 = \dfrac{28}{2} = 14$

Inter-quartile range (IQR)

The inter-quartile range is the difference between the upper quartile and lower quartile. It is a measure of dispersion and is used to describe the variability in a sample. It is usually used with the mean or median and tells us how well each represents the data.

Example using the median:

(Remember the median finds the middle number. The median divides the data into two halves, or into quartiles – lower and upper.)

7, 3, 6, 10, 9, 11, 5, 7, 9, 10, 12, 4

First we need to sort the data into order:

3, 4, 5, 6, 7, 7, 9, 9, 10, 10, 11, 12

The median = $7 + 9 = \dfrac{16}{2} = 8$

Inter-quartile range:

Table 2.30

Lower quartile					Median		Upper quartile				
3	4	5	6	7	7	9	9	10	10	11	12

You now have to find the median in both the lower and upper quartiles.

Lower quartile = 5

Upper quartile = 10

Inter-quartile range (IQR) = 10 − 5 = 5

Standard deviation

Standard deviation tells us how far values are from the average. The formula for working this out is the square root of the variance. The variance is the average of the squared differences from the mean.

To work out standard deviation:
- Find out what the mean is.
- For each number in the sample subtract the mean and square the results.
- Then work out the average of the squared differences.

Example:

The following data refers to the height in centimetres of ten students in a class.

156, 152, 157, 155, 161, 154, 145, 149, 147, 151

Mean height = 153

$156 - 153 = 3^2$

$152 - 153 = -1^2$

$157 - 153 = 4^2$

$155 - 153 = 2^2$

$161 - 153 = 8^2$

$154 - 153 = 1^2$

$145 - 153 = -8^2$

$149 - 153 = -4^2$

$147 - 153 = -6^2$

$151 - 153 = -2^2$

Variance $= 3^2 + -1^2 + 4^2 + 2^2 + 8^2 + 1^2 + -8^2 + -4^2 + -6^2 + -2^2 = \dfrac{216}{10} = 21.5$

Variance $= \sqrt{21.5}$

Variance $= 4.5$ cm

Activities

1   Using the information below, work out the mean class size of S1 students.

Table 2.31

Class	Class size
1C1	21
1C2	24
1E1	30
1E2	27
1K1	26
1K2	29
1L1	30
1L2	24
1W1	27
1W2	26

$\Rightarrow$

2 Using the same data, work out the mode.
3 Again, using the same information, work out the median.
4 What is the inter-quartile range?
5 Using standard deviation, what is the variance?
6 Using the information below, repeat questions 2–5.

Velocity of a river at various points along its course:

0.34, 0.27, 0.08, 0.19, 0.31, 0.07, 0.16, 0.26, 0.15, 0.14, 0.32, 0.09, 0.32, 0.09

Spearman's rank correlation coefficient

Spearman's rank correlation coefficient is a way of determining the strength of a relationship between two variables.

The result will always be shown between 1 and −1, with 1 being a perfect positive relationship and −1 being a perfect negative relationship.

Example

Begin by putting your results into table form.

In the example below, the two variables are 'Friction' and 'Velocity'.

Rank both the variables and input them into the correct column. In order to rank the data, award '1' to the highest number, then '2' etc., until you have awarded each value a number. If there are tied scores, such as at Sites 6 and 7 in the example below, you must find the mean. In this case it was rank 2 and 3 that were tied.

Therefore $2 + 3 = \dfrac{5}{2} = 2.5$

Work out the difference between ranks by subtracting the rank of the second variable from the first.

Square the differences (d^2) then add them together.

You can work out the relation using this formula:

$$(R) = 1 - \frac{6\sum d^2}{n^3 - n^1}$$

In the formula, n = the number of sites. In the example below, eight sites were visited.

Table 2.32

Site	Friction	Rank friction	Velocity	Rank velocity	Difference between ranks (d)	d^2
1	3	8	0.35	1	7	49
2	5	6	0.3	2	4	16
3	4	7	0.27	3	4	16

Table 2.32 (cont.)

Site	Friction	Rank friction	Velocity	Rank velocity	Difference between ranks (d)	d^2
4	6	5	0.23	4	1	1
5	7	4	0.21	5	−1	1
6	8	2.5	0.17	6	−3.5	12.25
7	8	2.5	0.11	7	−4.5	20.25
8	9	1	0.08	8	−7	49

$\sum d^2 = 164.5$

Coefficient $(R) = 1 - \dfrac{6\sum d^2}{n^3 - n}$

$R = 1 - \dfrac{6 \times 164.5}{8^3 - 8}$

$(R) = 1 - 1.95$

$R = -0.95$

In this example, there is a very strong negative correlation between friction and velocity of a river.

Activity

1 Copy and complete the table.

Table 2.33

Site	Velocity (mps)	Rank velocity	Depth (m)	Rank depth	Difference between ranks (d)
1	0.43		0.54		
2	0.39		0.46		
3	0.27		0.58		
4	0.22		0.77		
5	0.18		0.86		
6	0.13		0.99		
7	0.09		1.07		

2 Using the information in the table above and the formula shown below, work out the Spearman's rank correlation coefficient.

$(R) = 1 - \dfrac{6\sum d^2}{n^3 - n}$

Nearest neighbour

Nearest neighbour is used to determine the distribution of something, such as settlements or a type of land use, for example a shop, according to whether the data is shown as clustered, random or regular.

Nearest neighbour analysis is useful in many studies. The formula enables you to see how far apart things are.

The formula will give you a result between 0 and 2.15.

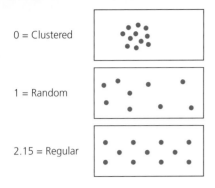

0 = Clustered

1 = Random

2.15 = Regular

Figure 2.31 Nearest neighbour analysis diagram

Example

The nearest neighbour formula is:

$$R_n = 2d \sqrt{\frac{n}{a}}$$

R_n = the nearest neighbour

d = the mean observed nearest neighbour distance

n = the total number of points

a = the total area

- Your study area must contain a minimum of 30 points.
- Measure the straight line distance between each point and its nearest neighbour. Table 2.34 below shows the distance between newsagents in the CBD.
- Next find the mean distance between the newsagents.
- Finally, work out the total area being studied.

According to these findings newsagents in this CBD are pretty random, as can be seen in Figure 2.32 which shows the range of random matching.

Table 2.34

Newsagent	Distance to nearest neighbour (m)
1	5.2
2	11.9
3	6.9
4	14.6
5	3.7
6	12.0
7	6.3
8	9.5
9	11.0
10	2.2
11	3.5
12	7.6
13	12.4
14	7.4
15	14.6
16	13.7
17	9.4

⇨

Table 2.34 (cont.)

Newsagent	Distance to nearest neighbour (m)
18	7.9
19	11.5
20	16.4
21	19.5
22	12.6
23	7.9
24	8.4
25	4.3
26	8.3
27	12.3
28	9.9
29	14.4
30	18.9
(mean) d = 10.14	
a = 3218 m	
$R_n = 2d \sqrt{\dfrac{n}{a}}$ $R_n = 2 \times 25.32 \sqrt{\dfrac{30}{3218}}$ $R_n = 10.14 \times 0.095$ $R_n = 0.96$	

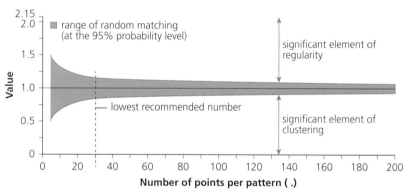

Figure 2.32 Range of random matching

Activity

Using the information in the table below, work out what the nearest neighbour is.

Table 2.35

Settlement	Distance to nearest neighbour (m)
1	3.7
2	2.1
3	3.8
4	1.9
5	5.2
6	3.7

$\Rightarrow$

Table 2.35 (cont.)

Settlement	Distance to nearest neighbour (m)
7	1.8
8	4.5
9	6.1
10	6.3
11	4.6
12	2.8
13	5.7
14	5.2
15	0.7
16	3.6
17	2.4
18	2.8
19	1.4
20	2.7
21	4.1
22	2.8
23	3.7
24	2.6
25	3.2
26	1.8
27	1.5
28	0.6
29	1.3
30	4.2
(mean) $d = 3.2$	
$a = 16093$ metres	
$R_n = 2d \sqrt{\dfrac{n}{a}}$	

Key words

Inter-quartile range: A way of measuring how spread out a set of data is.

Mean: Another word for 'average'.

Median: The middle number in a set of data.

Mode: The name given to a number that appears most often in a set of data.

Nearest neighbour: Used to determine the distribution of something, according to whether the data is shown as clustered, random or regular.

Spearman's rank correlation coefficient: A way of determining the strength of a relationship between two variables.

Standard deviation: Shows how far a set of values are from the average.

3.1
Glacial study

Choosing a title

Now that you have opted to carry out a glacial study, you must choose an appropriate title. For this, you must decide what aspect of glaciation you want to focus on, for example, are you going to look at a specific glaciated area in detail, or are you just going to focus on one specific aspect of glaciation, such as erosion? Does your study involve one particular glacial feature, or many? There is a lot to think about, so here are some ideas.

Things to consider

1 Are corries mainly found on the north-facing side of a mountain?
2 Does the size of a corrie depend on its height?
3 Is a drumlins lee slope always gentler than the stoss end?
4 Do drumlins always form in swarms?
5 Is the size and shape of scree related to the steepness of a slope?
6 Why are rocks of different geologies found in lowland areas?
7 How does the land use differ between an upland glaciated area and a lowland glaciated area?
8 Is tourism more popular in an upland glaciated area or a lowland glaciated area?
9 Using an Ordnance Survey map, investigate whether a valley has been formed by glaciation.
10 Using an Ordnance Survey map, investigate if an area has evidence of glaciation.

Top tip

Don't make your title too complicated otherwise you will confuse yourself and the marker.

Collecting evidence in the field

In the exam, you need to describe two research methods used to collect information about your chosen topic. However, in practice, you will probably have to carry out many more and you can choose two of your 'best' for the exam.

Before you start

Before you start your glacial study there are several things that you need to consider.

★ Choose a title.
★ Write down all the research methods you will need to carry out to fully investigate your title.
★ Write down all the equipment you will need.
★ Plan what area(s) you will need to visit.
★ Choose a suitable day(s) to carry out your investigation. Remember safety is the most important thing so don't carry out this research in an area that is known to be dangerous or on a day when the weather is poor.
★ Think about your processing techniques and how you will show the information that you have collected. If you plan to draw field sketches, why not use a camera/camera-phone to take photos that you can use to draw a field sketch from later rather than doing it on the day.

Glaciation theory

Upland glaciated areas

Examples of upland glaciated areas in Scotland are found in:

● North West Highlands
● Grampians/Cairngorms
● Loch Lomond.

Processes of erosion

Freeze-thaw weathering is a process which eventually leads to rocks and stones cracking and breaking off. It occurs when temperatures are constantly rising and falling above and below freezing. When temperatures are above 0° any precipitation that falls onto rock surfaces can trickle through the cracks in the rocks. When temperatures fall below 0° the water freezes and expands; this puts a lot of pressure on the surrounding rock. By day, when temperatures rise again, the ice melts, releasing the pressure. Freeze-thaw is a continuous process that weakens the rock, eventually causing it to crack and break off.

Plucking is a glacial process which occurs when a glacier moves. Glaciers freeze onto the rocks and stones on the surface. When the glacier moves due to gravity it tears the rocks and stones away from the surface, leaving it jagged and rough.

Abrasion is another process of glaciation. Rocks and stones that have been plucked from the surface become embedded inside the glacier. These rocks scrape against the rugged surface, like the action of sandpaper, causing it to become smooth. Abrasion creates smooth surfaces that often have scratch marks known as striations on them.

Features of erosion

Corries are one of the most common glacial features and are bowl-shaped hollows that are found high up on the hillside. Many corries form on the north-facing side of a hill, as this is where temperatures are coldest. Corries typically have a steep back wall and sides and a lip at the front. The base of the corrie tends to be deep as the glacier deepens it during glaciation by rotational movement. The lip is formed when the glacier temporarily loses energy and is forced to deposit some of the material it is carrying. Scree often builds up inside the corrie at the base of the back and sidewalls. This is because these areas are so steep, often resulting in loose rocks breaking off and falling to the base.

Tarns are also a feature of a corrie, although they are not always found there. Tarns are small areas of water that have collected inside the corrie after glaciation.

Arêtes occur when two corries form back-to-back or side-by-side on one hillside. The back wall and sides of the corries are eroded so that all that remains of the hillside is a steep, rocky ridge.

Pyramidal peaks are sharp peaks at the tip of a mountain. They are formed when three or more corries form back-to-back on one hillside.

U-shaped valleys are valleys that have two very steep sides, separated by a very flat base. These features are former V-shaped valleys which have become steeper and wider during glaciation. Quite often, the old river returns after glaciation and becomes known as a **misfit stream**. This is because the valley is far too wide for the narrow river that runs through it. Some U-shaped valleys are occupied by ribbon lakes. These are lakes that fill the base of U-shaped valleys. They form when the base of the U-shaped valley has been over deepened by glacial erosion.

Land uses

Farming in upland areas is mainly restricted to hill-sheep farming. The mountainous land means that soils are thin and infertile and the growing season is very short because of the height of the land. This means that arable farming would not be possible here. Some arable farming may be possible on the flat bases of the U-shaped valleys, where temperatures might be warmer and the land is much flatter.

Forestry is a popular land use in upland glaciated areas. The land here tends to be marginal and as it is not really possible to use the land for much else, forestry is quite often favoured.

Tourism is an important use of the land and many tourists visit upland glaciated areas every year. Tourists generally want to ramble or walk the hills; they might want to go rock climbing on some of the steeper land such as the pyramidal peaks. Skiing is popular in winter months, especially on the corries. The ribbon lakes can be used for water sports activities such as jet skiing and waterskiing and also for fishing and boat trips.

Water storage and supply is another important use. Ribbon lakes provide excellent, natural methods of storing water for nearby settlements. The high rainfall generally associated with upland areas makes this a reliable land use.

Renewable energy

Often hanging valleys and tarns are dammed to produce hydroelectric power. Wind turbines can be located in higher areas to produce wind power.

Land use conflicts and solutions

Table 3.1

Conflict	Solution
Forestry	
Hides scenery Rectilinear pattern spoils scenery Reduces diversity of flora and fauna Harbours pests Lorries cause congestion on the narrow roads	Use forest architects to design forests using a variety of trees and to highlight landforms Do not plant trees to the tops of the hillsides and avoid using straight lines Make agreements with specific organisations not to plant in the most scenic and popular areas
Tourism	
Congestion problems in honeypot areas Soil erosion reduces quality of farmland and looks unsightly Noisy pursuits conflict with quiet ones, e.g. waterskier and fishermen Farmers' gates are left open, allowing animals to escape Drop litter Often require costly specialist services such as mountain rescue	Zone leisure activities so that noisy pursuits cannot affect quieter ones Advertise other attractions that would divert people away from honeypot areas Educate tourists Employ wardens and rangers to monitor the area Widen major trunk roads where possible

Lowland glaciated areas

Features of deposition

Drumlins are small hills, with one steep side known as the stoss end, and a more streamlined slope, known as the lee slope. These features are made up of glacial till and are completely unsorted in their formation: the mound of moraine was just 'dumped' by the glacier when it ran out of energy. Drumlins can be up to one kilometre in length and over 50 m in height.

A drumlin's stoss end tends to be at the up-ice end, while the lee slope faces the direction the ice was moving in. Drumlins rarely occur singly and are generally found in groups, known as swarms.

Terminal moraines (sometimes known as **end moraines**) mark the furthest point reached by a glacier. These features are long ridges of completely unsorted material. They are small features, generally no higher than 20 m.

Erratics are rocks that are different in size and geology to the rock usually found in a particular area. These rocks were transported by the glacier, in some cases for hundreds of kilometres, and then left behind after the glacier melted.

Eskers are features of fluvioglacial deposition, which means that they were formed by melting ice rather than the ice itself. Eskers are long, sinuous ridges of sorted material. The reason why eskers are sorted is because they were formed by melt water, and water sorts material based on weight and size, with the larger, heavier material at the base and smaller, lighter material at the top. Eskers can run for tens of miles in length and can be one long, continuous piece or they may be broken in sections.

Outwash plains are another feature of fluvioglacial deposition and are broad plains of glacial sediments deposited by melt water. Any material that the glacier has been carrying on its journey that hasn't been previously deposited might be deposited here. Melt water carries this material and deposits it far away from the glacier snout. As the material is being transported by water, the material is sorted, with the larger boulders being deposited closest to the glacier and the finest materials being deposited furthest away.

Land uses

Arable farming is possible in lowland areas because the till deposits can make the land quite fertile. The milder temperatures allow for a reasonable growing season and the flat land means soils are relatively deep.

Dairy farming can also take place here as the temperatures are milder and the heavier clay soils may allow for good grass production.

Forestry is also a common land use in the lowland areas. Any land that is not good enough for farming may be used for forestry.

Quarrying is possible in lowland areas where there are outwash sands and gravels as these are useful for certain industries, particularly concrete industries.

Tourism is not as common in lowland areas as it is in upland areas because there are fewer recreational activities available. The features found in the lowlands are perhaps not as visually impressive as those in the upland areas and the lack of hills rules out many activities.

Land use conflicts and solutions

Table 3.2

Conflict	Solution
Quarrying	
Lorries transporting rock and stone cause congestion on narrow roads Quarries produce a lot of noise which can scare animals and annoy locals and tourists Quarries produce a lot of dust which can pollute water supplies Quarries can be unsightly and scar the landscape	Quarries can be screened off using trees Stone and rock could be transported by rail rather than road to reduce congestion

Key words

Abrasion: The process by which rocks within ice sheets scrape and erode the land over which they pass.

Arête: A narrow ridge between two corries, which occurs as the corries are formed on two adjacent sides of a mountain.

Corrie: A hollow on the side of a mountain, formed by ice filling a hollow and eroding the side of the mountain through abrasion and plucking and rotational movement at the base of the hollow.

Drumlin: An oval-shaped hill formed from deposits within a glacier.

Erratics: Rocks or boulders that have been moved by ice sheets from their original location and left in another location.

Eskers: Long ridges of sand and gravel deposited by rivers that flowed under ice sheets.

Freeze-thaw weathering: When water trapped in cracks in rocks alternately freezes and thaws, causing the rock to break up.

Misfit stream: A small river that occupies a U-shaped valley which was not the original river flowing through the valley.

Outwash plain: A wide plain of glacial sediments deposited by melt water.

Plucking: The process by which moving ice tears rocks from the surface over which it moves.

Pyramidal peaks: A jagged peak on top of a mountain.

Tarn: A small area of water which has collected inside a corrie after glaciation.

Terminal or end moraine: Material deposited by a glacier at the front of the glacier as it melts.

U-shaped valleys: A valley with two very steep sides and a wide flat base.

Example National 5 assignment
Processed Information

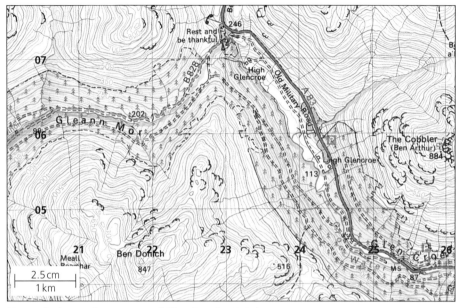

Map 1 Ordnance Survey map of Glen Croe (1:25000)

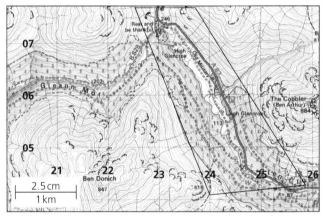

Map 2 Area being studied

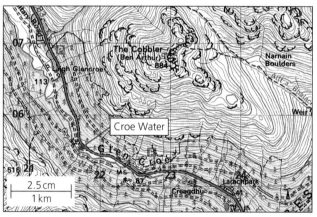

Map 3 Map of area 1:10000

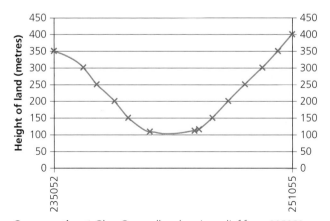

Cross-section 1 Glen Croe valley showing relief from 235052 to 251055

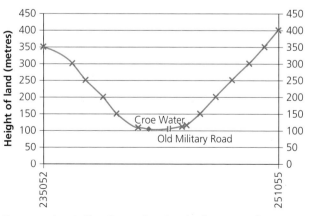

Cross-section 2 Glen Croe valley showing important features

Map extracts reproduced by permission © Crown copyright 2017 Ordnance Survey 100047450.

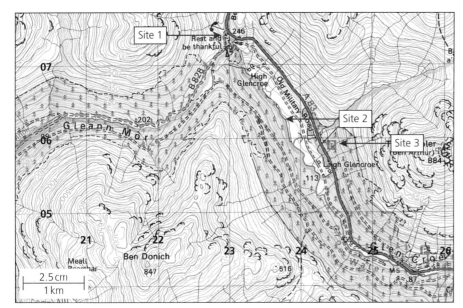

Table 1 Valley and river features

Slope angle of valley floor	8°
Valley floor width	122 m
River width	1.92 m
River depth	34 cm

Map 4 Map of Glen Croe showing location of Sites 1, 2 and 3

Photograph 1 View of Glen Croe from Rest and Be Thankful

Photograph 2 View of Glen Croe from Sheep Dip

Photograph 4 View of Glen Croe showing truncated spurs

Photograph 3 Scree on sidewalls

Map extract reproduced by permission © Crown copyright 2017 Ordnance Survey 100047450.

National 5 Geography assignment	
Candidate name:	Joe Bloggs

State the topic or issue you have researched

The aim of my assignment was to investigate, using an Ordnance Survey map, whether Glen Croe has been formed by glaciation.

Research methods (6 marks)

Describe two research methods you used to collect information about your topic or issue.

Location

Glen Croe is a valley in the Arrochar Alps near Loch Long and Loch Lomond. I chose to study this valley as I wanted to study somewhere that was accessible, which this valley is via the A83 and it was immediately identifiable using the OS Landranger Map of Loch Lomond and Inverary.

1 I gathered information from an OS map

Having decided to study Glen Croe, I used an Ordnance Survey (OS) map of Loch Lomond and Inverary to identify features of interest. The aim of my study was to investigate if Glen Croe was formed by glaciation; therefore I used the OS map to look for evidence of glaciation. I looked for evidence to support this theory that this is a glaciated valley, typically looking for steep sidewalls and a flat valley floor. I also looked to see if there were further glacial features that would bolster my argument such as hanging valleys, misfit streams and corries. After identifying any feature of interest I decided to use the OS map to draw a cross-section. Using the OS map of Loch Lomond and Inverary I chose two points where I wanted to start and finish the cross-section. To draw the shape of the valley I had to connect two points on either side. I didn't take each point to the highest peak, only to where the steepness of the land began to ease off. I placed a piece of plain paper along the cross-section line and marked the 6-figure grid references at the beginning and end. Moving along the cross-section line, I marked whenever a contour line crossed the paper. I also included the river, Croe Water and the Old Military Road as I thought these were important features. Once I had marked all of the contour lines I had to put it into a graph. I measured the distance between the two 6-figure grid references and made this the x axis of the graph. The y axis shows the height of the land. I placed the piece of plain paper with all the markings along the x axis and marked the height at that particular point. Once I had marked all the points, I joined them together to show the shape of the land. I then annotated it with the features mentioned.

2 I measured the slope angle

I chose a suitable location to measure the slope angle. From the OS map I decided to take this measurement in a central location along the valley and I decided on the area in Site 2. Before I went to the site I had to make my own clinometer using a protractor. At the site I used two metre sticks, one located on the bank of Croe Water looking west towards the A84, while the other metre stick was located at the top of the slope. I placed my clinometer at the top of the metre stick and angled it towards the top of the second metre stick. I recorded the reading on my record sheet.

Conclusions (14 marks)

For this section you must:

(i) Describe and explain, in detail, the main findings of your research.

(ii) State what conclusions you have reached about your topic or issue.

Description of findings

I chose Glen Croe in the Arrochar Alps shown in Map 1, as this appears to be a 'typical' U-shaped valley. From the OS map it has the traits that you would look for when identifying this feature, such as steep sidewalls and a flat valley floor as well as a misfit stream. Maps 2 and 3 further highlight the valley in question and the features are clearer using a smaller scale OS map in Map 3.

Cross-section 1 shows the shape of the land. From this cross-section, it is clear that the valley has a definite 'U' shape, with high steep sides ranging from 100 m on the valley floor to 350–400 m on either side of the valley.

Cross-section 2 highlights the river, Croe Water. It is clear from this cross-section as well as Map 1 that the river is far smaller than the valley. The river is very narrow and does not fill the broad valley floor, which is typical of a misfit stream.

The presence of the Old Military Road is also of some importance as it highlights that when the road was built in the 1700s, this was the 'easiest' route, where the land was flattest, rather than building the road on the steep sidewalls, where the A83 is now.

Map 4 shows the three sites that I chose to take photographs from and Photographs 1, 2 and 3 are the best pictures from each site, highlighting the shape of the valley sides and floor. Photograph 1 highlights the shape of the land well, showing a typical 'U' shaped cross-section. Photograph 2 shows the shape of the valley floor and the river's importance and Photograph 3 shows the build-up of scree on the slopes at the car park at Site 3.

Table 1 shows the slope angle along the valley floor measured at Sheep Dip (Photograph 2). From this it is clear that the valley floor is relatively flat with a gradient of only 8°. Also shown in Table 1 is the width of the valley floor, which was 122 m, the width of Croe Water which was 1.92 m and the average depth of the river which was 34 cm.

Explanation of findings

Cross-section 1 highlights the shape of the land and it is clear that the valley has two steep sidewalls on either side of a flat valley floor. This is the typical shape of a U-shaped valley. Before glaciation, Glen Croe would have been a V-shaped river valley, where Croe Water would likely have flowed. During glaciation the valley would have filled with snow and ice, eventually turning into a glacier. As the glacier moved down valley, huge amounts of rock would have been torn away from the valley sides, making them much steeper. Rocks and stones would also have been plucked away from the valley floor and scraped against the surface, making it much broader, smoother and flatter.

Cross-section 2, Map 1 and Photograph 1 all highlight the differences between the valley width and the river width. This is also evident from Table 1. The valley is far wider than the river running through it. This is because, before glaciation, when the river was a V-shaped river valley, the river would have 'fitted' this valley perfectly. It would be in the upper course and generally be very narrow and shallow. The valley sides would have been very steep. After glaciation, when the rocks and stones had been plucked away from the sides and base, the valley became much broader and flatter, but the river remains the same size. It is still in its upper course and therefore is still very narrow and shallow and no longer 'fits' the valley, which is why Croe Water is known as a misfit stream, which is a feature of glaciation.

Photographs 1, 2 and 3 further highlight the shape of the land, with Photograph 1 showing the view looking down the valley from the Rest and Be Thankful car park. The 'U' shaped cross-section is clear and you can see the direction the glacier would have been moving in. Scree is noticeable at the sides of the valley floor in Photograph 3, where constant rock falls have occurred. This is typical in a glaciated valley as the sides are so high and steep and susceptible to freeze-thaw weathering. Eventually the rocks break off and fall to the bottom of the slope where they shatter and build up small hills.

Conclusion

The aim of my assignment was to investigate, using an OS map, whether Glen Croe has been formed by glaciation. I chose six ways to test this: I drew a cross-section of the valley, took photographs, measured the slope angle of the valley floor, measured the width of the valley floor and measured the width and depth of Croe Water.

The results I got had no surprises and were really as I had expected. In order for my results to be more accurate, I could have selected a couple of sites along the valley floor to measure the width of the valley and found an average rather than just measuring at one site. This might have produced a more accurate result as it is clear from the OS maps and photographs that the valley floor varies in width. I also could have done the same with the river measurements, as by only measuring these features at one point, there may be 'freak' results. Potentially the river may be slightly narrower and shallower at this particular point than at other points along its course. Finding an average from two or three sites might have produced a more accurate reflection of the river, although had both of these been carried out, it would be unlikely to change the outcome of my study.

Glen Croe is a good example of a U-shaped valley, but I would have liked to see more features of glaciation. It was clear from the OS map that this was only a U-shaped valley and misfit stream; to strengthen my argument that this feature has been formed through glaciation, it would have been beneficial to see more features of glaciation such as a hanging valley or ribbon lake. These features also form from glaciation and therefore it would have bolstered my argument.

All the measurements were taken on the same day under the same weather conditions where there was no rain throughout the day.

Overall, it is possible to conclude that Glen Croe is a U-shaped valley that was formed by glaciation.

Don't forget – you only have one hour to write up your assignment!

3.2
River study

Choosing a title

Now that you have opted to carry out a river study, you must choose an appropriate title. For this, you must decide what aspect of the river you want to focus on, for example, are you going to look at the entire river from source to mouth? Or just one or two stages, such as the upper course and the lower course? Are you going to focus on one or two specific characteristics such as speed and depth or all of them? There is a lot to think about, so here are some ideas.

Things to consider

1 Does the speed of a river change from the upper course to the lower course?
2 How does the load of the river change downstream?
3 Does the river become more meandering downstream?
4 How do river characteristics change downstream?
5 How does land use change downstream?
6 Is there a relationship between the velocity of a river and its depth?
7 Do the uses of a river change downstream?
8 Is the size and shape of the bed load related to the velocity of a river?
9 How does the bed load change downstream?
10 Is the gradient of the valley the only factor that affects the speed of a river?

Top tip

Don't make your title too complicated otherwise you will confuse yourself and the marker.

Collecting evidence in the field

In the exam, you need to describe two research methods used to collect information about your chosen topic. However, in practice you will probably have to carry out many more and you can choose two of your 'best' for the exam.

Before you start

Before you go racing down to your nearest river to start your study, there are several things to think about.

What will you need to find out in order to answer your chosen title? For example, for idea 1 – *Does the speed of the river change from the upper course to the lower course?* – you will need to do the following:

★ Choose a title.
★ Write down all the research methods you will need to carry out to fully investigate your title.
⇨

⇒
- ★ Choose an 'appropriate' river – one that is not too wide or too deep as you will need to wade into it to carry out your research.
- ★ Find out where the source and mouth of the river is and all the different stages.
- ★ Be confident at how to measure the speed of a river as well as any calculations that may need to be done, such as working out the velocity in metres per second.
- ★ Decide how many sites you want to include and where.
- ★ Look at other factors that may/may not affect the speed of the river such as width, depth and gradient of land and know how to measure these.
- ★ Choose a suitable day(s) to carry out your investigation. Remember safety is the most important consideration, so don't carry out this research on a river that is known to be dangerous or following very heavy rainfall. Heavy rainfall will obscure your results too.
- ★ Make sure you have all the necessary equipment that you will need such as tape measures, metre sticks, stopwatch, tangerines, etc.
- ★ Think about your processing techniques and how you will show the information that you have collected. If you plan to draw field sketches, why not use a camera/camera-phone to take photos that you can use to draw a field sketch from later rather than doing it on the day.

Measuring and recording river characteristics

How to measure the velocity of a river

The velocity of a river is the speed at which the water flows through it.

Equipment required

- ☞ Stopwatch
- ☞ Tape measure
- ☞ Floating object such as a tangerine
- ☞ Record sheet
- ☞ Pen/pencil
- ☞ Clipboard
- ☞ Markers

Method

1 Using the tape measure, measure a 10-metre stretch along the riverbank. Mark the start and finish using markers.
2 Place the tangerine in the river just upstream of your starting point.
3 When the tangerine reaches the starting point, start the stopwatch.
4 Time how long it takes the tangerine to reach the finishing point.

5 Record your findings.
6 Repeat this five times.
7 Calculate the average speed of the river. For example:
  If you measured the speed of the river five times over a distance of 10 metres and got the following results:
  a) 26 seconds
  b) 29 seconds
  c) 27 seconds
  d) 32 seconds
  e) 31 seconds
  To find the average you add the results together and divide by the number of times you carried out the method.

  $\text{Average} = \dfrac{145}{5} = 29 \text{ seconds}$

  In order to work out the speed of the river in metres per second, use the following calculation.

  $\text{Speed} = \dfrac{\text{Distance}}{\text{Time}}$

  $\text{Speed} = \dfrac{10}{29} = 0.34 \text{ metres per second}$

Things to consider

Depending on what your study is, you may also want to measure the speed at three points across the river, i.e. at the left bank, middle and right bank.

Example: Measuring velocity over 10 m

Table 3.3

Attempt	1	2	3	4	5
Speed (seconds)	26	29	27	32	31
Speed (cumecs)	0.38	0.34	0.37	0.31	0.32

Top tip

Remember! Cumecs are cubic metres per second.

How to measure the depth of a river

The depth of a river is the distance from the riverbed to the surface of the river.

Equipment required

☞ Tape measure
☞ Metre stick
☞ Record sheet
☞ Pen/pencil
☞ Clipboard

Method

1 Two people will need to hold the measuring tape across the river.
2 Using the metre stick, measure the depth of the river across the stream every 30 to 50 cm intervals.
3 Record your findings.

Things to consider

Depending on your study, you may want to find the average depth using the information you have collected.

Example: Measuring depth

Table 3.4

Distance across the river (m)	0	0.5	1.0	1.5	2	2.5
Depth (m)	0.89	0.76	0.73	0.69	0.76	0.81

How to measure the width of a river

The width of the river is the distance across the river from one bank to the other.

Equipment required

☞ Tape measure
☞ Record sheet
☞ Pen/pencil
☞ Clipboard

Method

1 Stretch the tape measure taut across the river channel.
2 Record your findings.

Things to consider

1 Depending on your study, you may want to find out the width of the current water level or the bank-full width.
2 To measure the current width, keep the measuring tape taut just above the water level and measure across the river stream.
3 To measure the bank-full width, identify the point where the bank and vegetation suggest maximum capacity before the river would burst its banks and flood, then measure directly across that part of the river.

How to measure the wetted perimeter (in the field)

The wetted perimeter is the surface of the channel at the riverbanks and bed that are in direct contact with water.

Equipment required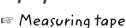

- ☞ Measuring tape
- ☞ Record sheet
- ☞ Pen/pencil
- ☞ Clipboard

Method

1 Use a tape measure to measure from the riverbed to the surface of the water at either side of the riverbank.
2 Record your findings.
3 Use a tape measure to measure the width across the riverbed. You will need to weigh your tape measure down with rocks to keep it in place.
4 Record your findings.
5 Now add up your findings from the riverbed and both banks.

Things to consider

1 This could be difficult to do in practice, especially if the river is flowing very quickly or is very deep or wide.
2 You might prefer to work out the wetted perimeter using a cross-section of the river (Figure 3.1) and this is described later in this section.

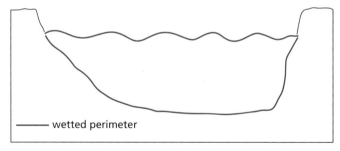
wetted perimeter

Figure 3.1 Wetted perimeter

How to measure friction (in the field)

Friction is created when there is resistance between the flowing water and the large boulders and rocks on the riverbed.

Equipment required

- ☞ Friction table
- ☞ Record sheet
- ☞ Pen/pencil
- ☞ Clipboard

Things to consider

1 There are two different types of friction – internal and external.
2 Internal friction can also be referred to as **turbulence**. This can be seen by looking at the river to see how calm or rough it is flowing. If the water is flowing very smoothly, there will be very little friction, whereas if the river appears to be quite choppy and rough with white water and rapids, then there is a lot of friction present.
3 External friction is friction that occurs when the water comes into contact with the riverbed and banks. If the riverbed and banks are very rough, with many tree roots, boulders and protruding rocks, external friction will be high and the surface of the river will probably appear choppy and turbulent. On the other hand, if the riverbed and banks are smooth, there will be far less friction and the surface of the river will appear calm.
4 Both methods of friction are worked out using a friction table.

Method

1 Look at the river to assess how it is flowing. Using the friction table, give the river an internal friction mark. Then by the same process, give the river an external friction mark. It may be difficult to see the riverbanks and bed so you may have to feel along the surfaces to check for tree roots and protruding rocks.
2 Repeat this at each site.
3 Add the internal friction mark to the external friction mark. The higher the mark, the more friction there is.

Table 3.5 Friction table

Internal friction		External friction	
Mark	What to look for	Mark	What to look for
1	Very calm water	1	Smooth bed, silt, no weeds or tree roots.
2	Differences in speed across the channel	2	Fairly smooth bed, sandy and no weeds
3	Some white water	3	Undulating bed, some weeds, sand and gravel
4	Mostly white water, especially around large boulders	4	Irregular bed, weeds, coarse gravel
5	Severe white water and rapids	5	Very irregular bed, many weeds, large boulders

Example: Measuring friction

Table 3.6

Site	Internal friction mark	External friction mark	Index of friction
1	4	5	9
2	4	4	8
3	3	4	7
4	2	3	5
5	1	2	3

How to measure the sinuosity of a river

The sinuosity of a river is how meandering or bendy it is.

Equipment required

☞ Measuring tape
☞ Record sheet
☞ Pen/pencil
☞ Clipboard
☞ Markers

Method

1 Choose a meander that you want to measure.
2 Put a marker at the start of the meander (point A).
3 Put a marker halfway round the bend (point B).
4 Put a marker at the end of the meander (point C).
5 Mark a point (1) halfway round between point A and point B.
6 Mark a point (2) halfway round between point B and point C.
7 Measure the distance straight across between points 1 and 2.
8 Measure the distance around the meander from points 1 to 2.
9 Use the following calculation to work out the sinuosity:

$$\text{Sinuosity} = \frac{\text{Distance between 1 and 2 around the meander}}{\text{Distance between 1 and 2 in a straight line}}$$

10 The closer the number is to 1, the straighter the river. This is called the index of sinuosity.

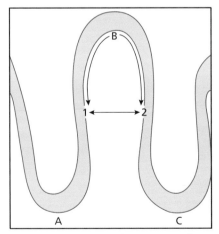

Figure 3.2 Measuring the sinuosity of a river

Processing information from results

The following methods of gathering information do not need to be carried out in the field but you will need the raw data that you collected.

How to draw a cross-section

A cross-section is a useful technique to show the shape and morphology of the river.

Equipment required

☞ Graph paper
☞ Ruler
☞ Pen/pencil
☞ Information collected in the field

Method

1 Study the information you collected on the depth of the river.
2 Use a suitable scale for the x and y axes.
3 The x axis shows the width across the river and the y axis shows the depth of the river.
4 Plot the depth of the river against the width across, as shown in Figure 3.3.
5 Join the dots together to show an outline of the river.

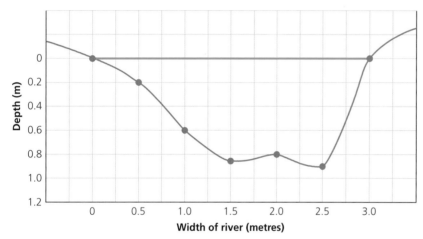

Figure 3.3 Cross-section of a river

How to calculate the wetted perimeter

Equipment required

☞ Piece of thread
☞ Ruler

Method

1 At the cross-section of the river, place the piece of thread at 0 (the surface of the river).
2 Follow the outline of the riverbank and bed, being careful not to move the start of the thread.
3 Continue to do this all the way round the river outline to the opposite bank.
4 Using a ruler measure the length of the thread used.
5 Use the scale to work out the wetted perimeter.

How to calculate the cross-sectional area

Equipment required
- ☞ Information collected in the field
- ☞ Calculator

Method
The following calculation will give you the cross-sectional area of a river.

Cross-sectional area = Average depth × Width

Example: Calculating the cross-sectional area
Cross-sectional area = 1.2 × 3 = 3.6 m² cross-sectional area

How to calculate the discharge of a river

Equipment required
- ☞ Information collected in the field
- ☞ Calculator

Method
The following calculation will give you the discharge of the river.

Discharge = Cross-sectional area × Average speed

Example: Calculating the discharge of a river
Discharge = 3.6 × 0.34 = discharge of 1.2 cumecs

How to calculate the efficiency ratio and friction

Equipment required
- ☞ Cross-sectional area of the river results
- ☞ Wetted perimeter results
- ☞ Index of friction results
- ☞ Calculator

Method

The following calculation will give you the efficiency ratio of the river:

$$\text{Efficiency ratio} = \frac{\text{Cross-sectional area}}{\text{Wetted perimeter}}$$

Example: Calculating the efficiency ratio

$$\text{Efficiency ratio} = \frac{3.6}{6} = 0.6 \text{ efficiency ratio}$$

The greater the efficiency ratio, the more efficient the river is.

The following calculation will tell you how much friction is acting on the river and therefore how efficient it is:

$$\text{Amount of friction acting on a river} = \frac{\text{Index of friction}}{\text{Efficiency ratio}}$$

Example: Calculating the amount of friction acting on a river

$$\text{Amount of friction acting on a river} = \frac{9}{0.6} = 15$$

In this case, the lower the number, the less friction there is, so the river must be more efficient.

Rivers theory

Upper course

Relief of river valley

Most rivers begin in upland areas. Where a river starts is known as its source. The relief of the land here is very steep.

Discharge

The volume of water in the river channel is low in the upper course as the river is in its youth and the channel is very narrow and shallow.

Friction

Friction is greatest in the upper course as the riverbed is full of large, angular rocks and boulders.

Velocity

The velocity of the river in the upper course is slower than in the other stages. This is largely to do with the friction that is generated here.

Energy

The river has limited energy here, which is again due to friction. Approximately 95 per cent of a river's energy is lost due to friction.

Width and lateral erosion

The upper course of the river is where the river has started, so it has not had time to complete much lateral **erosion** of the riverbanks; therefore the river is very narrow in the upper course.

Depth and vertical erosion

The river uses most of its energy to erode the riverbed at this stage (vertical erosion). The river is shallow but it is slowly eroding the channel.

Load

In the upper course the river is transporting very large, angular rocks and boulders. The rocks are like this because the river has not yet eroded them.

Hydraulic action, attrition and corrasion

Hydraulic action is when the force of the water hits the sides and base of the river, causing them to weaken and break up. This process is common in the upper course, particularly in the formation of waterfalls.

Attrition is the wearing down of the load as the rocks, stones and pebbles hit off each other. This makes them smooth and more rounded. This is less active in the upper course because at this stage the river is mainly carrying large rocks.

Corrasion is when the rocks and stones that the river transports hit off the banks and bed, causing them to break down. As the load is mainly large rocks and boulders, this process is not as common in the upper course.

Erosion, transportation and deposition

In the upper course, most of the river's energy is being used to erode vertically.

Transportation in the upper course is mainly by traction, where large rocks and stones are rolled or dragged along the riverbed by the force of the water.

There is very little deposition taking place at this stage.

River features

The main features of the river course at this stage are V-shaped valleys and waterfalls. **V-shaped valleys** are the steep sided valleys formed by vertical erosion. Waterfalls are areas where the geology of the rock is changing and so erosion produces vertical drops.

Land uses

The land in the upper course is so steep that there are very few opportunities for land uses. The land is mainly used for farmland, but is restricted to hill-sheep farming as it is too high and cold and the soil is too infertile to grow crops. Also, it is difficult to use machinery in upland areas. Sheep are happy grazing the land here.

Because of the cold weather, poor soils and steep slopes, land in the upper course may also be used for forestry.

Because V-shaped valleys are fairly easy to dam, reservoirs may be created in the upper course of the river.

How the river is used

The fast flowing water and steep slopes mean that opportunities for using the river here are limited. Recreational activities are perhaps the most common uses of the river. Kayaking, white-water rafting and canoeing are all popular at this stage. There is, however, an opportunity to generate hydroelectric power at this stage. The steep slopes and high rainfall can provide fast flowing water that can be used to generate electricity.

Middle course

Relief of river valley

As the river moves into its middle course, the land becomes less steep and is more undulating.

Discharge

The discharge of the river is higher at this stage as the channel is now wider and deeper, and so able to carry more water, but also because many tributary rivers have joined the river.

Friction

Friction is lower at this stage as the shape and size of the load is now smaller and more rounded, creating less friction.

Velocity

The river is flowing more quickly at this stage; this is because there is a higher discharge and less friction.

Energy

The river has more energy at this stage as the volume and speed of the river has increased. However, most of this energy is being used to transport a lot of materials.

Width and lateral erosion

Lateral erosion of the riverbanks has made the river a lot wider at this stage than in the upper course.

Depth and vertical erosion

The riverbed has been eroded vertically, which has made the river much deeper at this stage than in the upper course.

Load

The river has been eroding a lot of the material it has been carrying at this stage, so the load is much less angular than it was in the upper course. At this stage, mainly sub-angular and sub-rounded rocks will be found.

Hydraulic action, attrition and corrasion

Hydraulic action and corrasion are eroding the sides and base of the river channel. They are also helping to form some of the river features found in the middle course. The process of attrition has helped to smooth the load to the sub-angular and sub-rounded shapes.

Erosion, transportation and deposition

The river is carrying a lot more load at this stage so has less energy to erode.

In the middle course, the river is less able to move large rocks but carries most of its load either by saltation, which is when small stones bounce along the riverbed, or by suspension, when particles are small enough to be carried by the water.

The loss of energy also means that the river deposits the large boulders and rocks that it has been transporting from the upper course at this stage.

River features

Features of the middle course are mainly features of both erosion and deposition. Features of erosion produced at this stage include bends in the river, known as **meanders**, and river cliffs that form steep banks in the outside bend of the meander. Depositional features include river beaches and **braiding**. River beaches form on the inside bend of a meander and braiding, when the river deposits **alluvium** across the riverbed.

Land uses

As the land is less steep here, a wider variety of farming can take place. Arable farming can take place on the valley floor, which tends to be a bit flatter, while soils are more fertile and the weather is better. There will still be some livestock farming taking place on the lower slopes.

Some small settlements can be built on the flat valley floor and communications, such as roads and railways, are possible too.

How the river is used

The river itself may be used for recreational activities such as angling at this stage. The slower currents mean that fishing is more viable.

Lower course

Relief of river valley

The land is very flat at this stage of the river course.

Discharge

The volume of water flowing through the river channel in the lower course is at its highest. The river channel is very wide and very deep, so can hold a lot of water, and the river has been joined by many tributary rivers.

Friction

Friction is considerably less here as the size and shape of the load is much smaller and more rounded.

Velocity

Due to the volume of water flowing through the river channel and the absence of friction, the river is flowing fastest here and is flowing more efficiently.

Energy

Energy is greatest in the lower course due to the increased discharge and velocity. The excess energy is mainly being used to transport the river's load.

Width and lateral erosion

There has been a lot of lateral erosion of the riverbanks and so the river itself is very wide at this stage.

Depth and vertical erosion

The riverbed has also been eroded by vertical erosion so the river is very deep at this stage of the river course.

Load

The small stones and particles that the river carries here are all rounded and well rounded. The load of the river is greatest at this stage.

Hydraulic action, attrition and corrasion

These processes are limited here other than during times of flood, where the river has excess energy.

Erosion, transportation and deposition

Very little erosion takes place in the lower course, other than during times of flood, when the river has more energy due to the higher discharge of the river.

Transportation at this stage is mainly by suspension and solution. Solution is when the river dissolves minerals from the rocks at the banks and bed and carries them in the water itself.

River features

Most of the landforms found in the lower course have been formed by deposition. **Oxbow lakes**, which are very wide meanders that have been cut off from the main river, are common in the lower course. The flat land found on either side of the river channel, known as a floodplain, is found at this stage. **Levees** are also found; these are natural embankments made of deposited material found on either side of the river channel.

Land uses

The warmer temperatures and fertile soils from the alluvium deposited on the floodplain makes arable farming very profitable in the lower course. The flat land also allows farmers to use machinery.

Industry is also possible in the lower course as the wide, flat valley floor means that it is easy to build on. This is also the reason why large towns and cities are found at this stage.

Roads, railways and communications are all much more viable at this stage, again, due to the flat valley floor.

How the river is used

The river in the lower course is very deep and very wide and therefore it is possible to use the river as a means of transportation. Large ships and barges can sail along the river easily at this stage.

Keywords

Alluvium: The material deposited by a river, usually over its floodplain.

Braiding: The process by which a river divides into separate channels as a result of material being deposited by the river mid-stream.

Erosion: The process by which rocks are worn away.

Levees: Natural embankments made of deposited material, found on either side of the river channel.

Meanders: Bends formed in the middle or lower course of a river.

Oxbow lake: A lake formed by meanders where the top of the loop of the meander is cut off from the main channel, as the river finds a new, more direct path.

V-shaped valleys: A narrow valley, which is typically found in the upper stage of river development.

Example Higher assignment

Processed Information

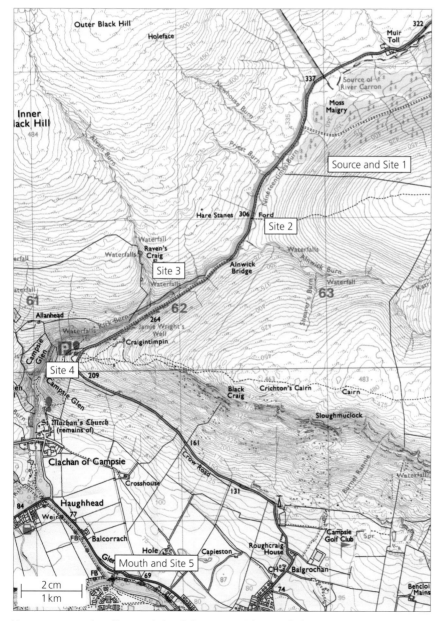

Map 1 Nineteentimes Burn, Campsie Fells

Map extract reproduced by permission © Crown copyright 2017 Ordnance Survey 100047450

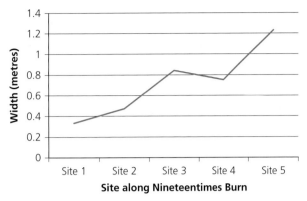

Graph 1 Width of Nineteentimes Burn

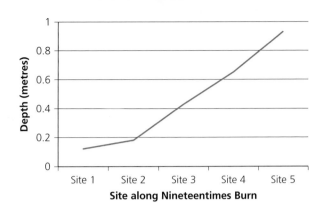

Graph 2 Depth of Nineteentimes Burn

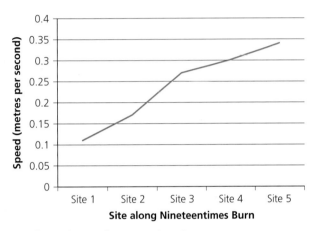

Graph 3 Velocity of Nineteentimes Burn

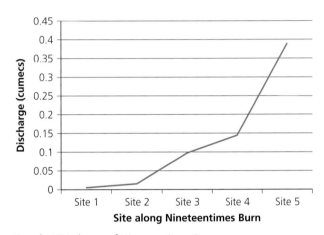

Graph 4 Discharge of Nineteentimes Burn

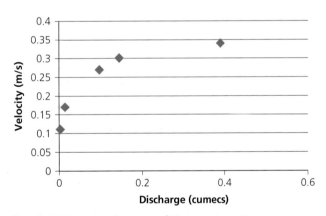

Graph 5 Velocity vs discharge of Nineteentimes Burn

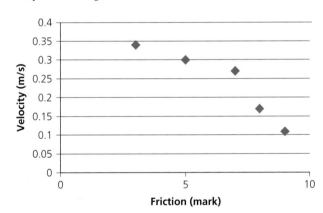

Graph 6 Velocity vs friction of Nineteentimes Burn

Table 1 Bed load

Site	1	2	3	4	5
Average size (cm)	31	23	17	11	7
Average shape	Very angular	Angular	Sub-angular	Sub-rounded	Rounded

Table 2 Friction

Site	Internal friction mark	External friction mark	Index of friction
1	4	5	9
2	4	4	8
3	3	4	7
4	2	3	5
5	1	2	3

Higher Geography assignment	
Candidate name:	Joe Bloggs

Introduction

Knowledge and understanding of the topic.

The aim of my assignment was to investigate how river characteristics – velocity, depth, width and bed load – change downstream.

The velocity, depth, width and bed load are four of the most important characteristics in a river. It is possible to make assumptions about these before conducting the investigation. The Bradshaw model describes how the river's characteristics should change between the source and the mouth. From the model, I would expect the river's velocity to increase downstream. I would assume this as, in any 'normal' river the velocity is slowest in the upper course where there is the least energy, and fastest in the lower course where the river has the most energy and force. However, as it may not be enough to consider only the velocity, I will also look at discharge of the river and friction as both of these can affect the velocity. Again, in terms of the depth of the river, I would expect that the river's depth increases downstream, as I know that vertical erosion increases downstream, therefore so should the depth of the river. This is similar to width. Lateral erosion is more common in the middle and lower courses; therefore, the width of the river should increase downstream. The bed load of the river should be larger and more angular in the upper course where there has been less opportunity for the rocks and boulders to be eroded by the river compared to the lower course. With all these characteristics there will be other factors that may or may not affect the results.

To complete the investigation I chose the Nineteentimes Burn in the Campsies. This is quite shallow and narrow and so practical and safe to use, except near its mouth, but it is long enough to have different stages. The Burn has a steep upper course in the hills, a short middle course as it leaves the hills and quite a long lower course in the lowlands before joining the Glazert Water. The research was carried out during one dry day in August 2016. It is important that all of these measurements are taken on the same day under the same weather conditions as if there is a period of rainfall throughout the day, the measurements can be obscured.

Research methods

A description of the research methods used and/or evaluation of the usefulness and/or reliability of any technique or sources used.

I selected five sites along the course of the Nineteentimes Burn. There were two sites from each stage of the river course other than in the lower course as the river was becoming too wide and deep to be safely measured. Sites 1 and 2 were in the upper course, Sites 3 and 4 were in the middle course and Site 5 was in the lower course. In retrospect, it would have been better to have two sites in each course, as this would have produced more consistency downstream.

Research method 1: Measuring Velocity

The first method I used was to measure the velocity of the river. Using a tape measure I measured a known distance along the riverbank. The distance varied depending on the stage of the river. In Sites 1 and 2 it was only possible to use a five-metre stretch, as the river is narrower and therefore had more obstacles in its path. For Sites 3, 4 and 5 a ten-metre distance was used. I placed a tangerine into the centre of the river just upstream from the starting point so that I had a bit of time before starting the stopwatch. I began timing as soon as the tangerine flowed past the starting position and timed how long it took to cover the distance measured out. I repeated this five times at each site to work out the average velocity at each site. It gives more accurate results using an average rather than just using one test as you may get a 'freak' result. From these results I calculated the speed in terms of metres per second, by dividing the distance by the speed. It was necessary to do this as different distances had been used, so in order to compare the speeds accurately, they needed to be in the same format.

Research method 2: Estimating friction

There is no experiment as such for assessing friction in a river. There are two types of friction, internal and external. Both are measured visually. Internal friction is also known as turbulence and can be assessed by looking at the river to see how calm or rough it is flowing. External friction occurs when the water comes into contact with the riverbed and banks. If the riverbed and banks are very rough with many tree roots, boulders and protruding rocks, external friction will be high and most likely the surface will appear choppy and turbulent. On the other hand, if the riverbed and banks are smooth, there will be far less friction and the surface will appear calm. ⇨

In order to measure both internal and external friction, I used a friction table. At each site along the river, I looked to see how rough or calm the water flowed and awarded the river a mark between 1 and 5, with 1 being calm and therefore least friction and 5 the roughest and therefore the most friction. To measure external friction, I was able to do this mainly by looking in the river itself to see whether there were many tree roots and boulders, and again a mark was given between 1 and 5. Where the river was cloudier, particularly at Site 3, I had to feel along the riverbed and banks to feel channel roughness. I recorded all of these marks on my record sheet. I was then able to add internal friction marks to external marks to give each site a total.

Estimating friction is not very accurate as it is not possible to see the river below the surface and it relies on my subjective judgement.

Analysing findings

Using the Processed Information to analyse the information.

As you can see in Graph 1, the width of the river became wider downstream, ranging from 0.33 m at Site 1 to 1.23 m at Site 5, almost four times as wide. Site 1 was in the upper course and Site 5 was in the lower course. This is typical of a river as the processes of erosion are wearing down the banks of the river channel. Hydraulic action, where the force of the water erodes the banks of the river by its sheer force, is most powerful in the middle and lower courses. So too, is the process of corrasion, where the rocks and stones being carried by the river are thrown against the sides and base, eroding them further. These processes will cause the river to become wider downstream.

Graph 2 shows the depth of the river. It is clear that between Site 1 in the upper course and Site 5 in the lower course, the river becomes much deeper. At Site 1 the river was 0.12 m deep and by Site 5 this had increased nearly eight times, to 0.93 m. This is due to vertical erosion. Vertical erosion is the downward erosion of the riverbed. It is caused by hydraulic action and corrasion. These processes are active in all stages of the river course but are most rapid in the middle and lower courses, where the river has more energy for this.

As you can see from Graph 3, the velocity of the river increases downstream. At Site 1 the velocity of the river was 0.11 metres per second whereas at Site 5 this had trebled its speed to 0.34 metres per second. This was something that I had anticipated as the speed of a river is slowest in the upper course, where there is a low discharge and greater friction created by the large, angular boulders found along the riverbed, as shown in Tables 1 and 2. The speed increases downstream, where the discharge increases, due to tributaries joining the river such as Newhouse Burn and Priest Burn. Friction decreases due to the smaller, more rounded nature of the load and channel. Graph 4 shows that the discharge of the Nineteentimes Burn did increase between Site 1 and Site 5 and Table 2 shows that friction decreased from 9 at Site 1 to 3 at Site 5. There is a positive relationship between velocity and discharge, shown in Graph 5. This means that as the discharge of the river increases, so does the velocity. This is because the sheer volume of water flowing through the river channel means relatively little is in contact with the bed and sides, which would slow it down. It is also clear from Graph 6 that there is a negative relationship between velocity and friction. As friction increases, the velocity of the river decreases. This is because where there are many obstacles in the river, such as large boulders, tree roots and weeds, these create resistance and the water is unable to flow smoothly past these obstacles.

The bed load, shown in Table 1, follows a similar predicable path. It was expected that the load of the river would be large and angular at Sites 1 and 2 where the river is in its upper course, becoming smaller and more rounded downstream, and this was exactly the case. The load tends to be smaller in the lower course because the river does not have the energy to transport such large rocks, as it is carrying a large volume of smaller materials in suspension and solution. The load also becomes more rounded, as the process of attrition, where stones and pebbles hit off each other causing them to become smoother (like the action of sandpaper), is more active. There may, of course, be some anomalies in this, for example, if a small tributary river joins the main river, much of its load may not have been eroded down yet, so larger, more angular rocks may be found further downstream than you would expect.

Conclusions
Reach a conclusion, supported by a range of evidence.
The aim of my assignment was to investigate how river characteristics – velocity, depth, width and bed load – change downstream. I chose five sites in order to test this. I didn't get any unexpected results in my investigation. All the measurements were as I expected, based on my understanding of a river's long profile. The width of the river increased downstream due to lateral erosion of the riverbanks caused by hydraulic action and corrasion. This was also true of the river depth, which also increased downstream, due to vertical erosion of the riverbed. The speed of the river increased in relation to the discharge of the river and the reduction of friction in the river channel. Finally, the bed load of the river became smaller and more rounded downstream as the agents of erosion wore the load down over time. Overall, it is safe to say that the characteristics of the Nineteentimes Burn – velocity, depth, width and bed load – do change downstream. The river behaves like a typical river. To test this further, I could have investigated other characteristics such as the river's straightness, and even its gradient, and used more sites to do this.

Don't forget – you only have 1 hour and 30 minutes to write up your assignment!

3.3
Weather study

Choosing a title

Now that you have opted to carry out a weather study, you must choose an appropriate title. For this, you must decide what aspect of the weather you want to focus on, for example, are you going to look at a specific element of the weather? Are you going to compare one or two weather elements or is your investigation going to focus on something more large scale such as the passing of a depression? There is a lot to think about, so here are some ideas:

Things to consider

1 Does wind speed depend on air pressure?
2 Is there a relationship between cloud cover and type and rainfall amount?
3 Do air temperatures vary more than ground temperatures?
4 Is there more rain with low air pressure?
5 How does temperature change during a depression?
6 How does rainfall differ at a warm and cold front?
7 How does the weather change during a depression?
8 How does wind speed change during a depression?
9 Does it matter where you locate weather instruments when recording the weather?
10 Are weather forecasts reliable?

Top tip

Don't make your title too complicated otherwise you will confuse yourself and the marker.

Collecting evidence in the field

In the exam, you need to describe two research methods used to collect information about your chosen topic. However, in practice you will probably have to carry out many more and you can choose two of your 'best' for the exam.

Before you start

Before you start your weather study there are several things to think about.

★ Choose a title.
★ Write down all the research methods you will need to carry out to fully investigate your title.
★ Write down all the equipment you will need.
★ If you are making weather instruments, make sure you have everything you need and have decided where to locate them.
★ If you will need to carry out studies on more than one day, plan this carefully.
★ If your study involves fronts and depressions, make sure you watch the weather forecast in advance to find out when one is likely.

How to measure the temperature

Temperature is how warm or cool either the air or ground temperature is.

Equipment required

☞ Thermometer
☞ Stevenson screen – wood or plastic box, white paint, Blu Tack
☞ Record sheet

Method

Temperature is usually measured using a Stevenson screen, but it is unlikely you will have access to one of these for your study. A Stevenson screen is a white box that contains thermometers that are used to measure the air temperature. By keeping these delicate instruments inside a wooden box, it protects them from obstruction or harm. Every day the temperature can be recorded by reading the results on the thermometer.

For the purpose of your study, you should be able to simply use a thermometer – a mercury or digital one will be fine. If you want to make your own Stevenson screen it is simple enough to do:

1   Take a wooden or plastic box.
2   Make several cuts/slits in it so that air can circulate.
3   Paint the box white (white reflects sunlight so the box won't overheat).
4   Using Blu Tack, stick the thermometer to the back wall.

You need to find a suitable location for your thermometer/Stevenson screen:

- It must be raised above ground (approximately 1 m above ground is sufficient – this means that it will not be affected by ground temperatures).
- It should be kept in the shade. If the sun shines directly on it the results will be misleading.
- It should be kept on a grassy surface, as concrete surfaces attract more heat, obscuring the results.
- There should be no obstructions blocking the thermometer so it is important to keep it clear of trees and buildings.
- Once you have found a suitable location for your thermometer/ Stevenson screen, recording the temperature is very straight forward.

Record the reading on the thermometer at the same time each day.

Record your reading on your record sheet.

Things to consider !

In order to make your findings more accurate, you may want to use maximum and minimum thermometers.

How to measure precipitation

Precipitation is any form of moisture that falls to the ground.

Equipment required

- ☞ Collecting cup/funnel
- ☞ Measuring jug
- ☞ Record sheet

Method

Rainfall is measured using a rain gauge. A rain gauge is just a cylinder that is put outside to collect any precipitation. You need to find a suitable location for your rain gauge:

1. The rain gauge must be raised above ground, to prevent surface water falling into the container.
2. The rain gauge must be placed on a vegetated or grassy surface; if it is placed on a surface such as tarmac, rain splashes might get into the container, obscuring results.
3. The gauge should be placed away from buildings and trees, in an open space, so that it is not sheltered.

Things to consider !

Try to record the rainfall as soon after a shower as possible, as the moisture might evaporate if it is left for too long.

How to measure wind direction

Wind direction is the direction that the wind is blowing from.

Equipment required

- ☞ Wind vane located on a nearby church or school
- ☞ Or materials to make a wind vane (scissors, straw, thick card, sticky tape, polystyrene cup with lid, pencil, a pin, stones, compass)
- ☞ Record sheet

Method

Wind direction is measured using a wind vane – these can be simple or complex. The most simple wind vane is an arrow attached to a pole and when the wind blows the arrow points in the direction the wind is blowing to. Very often you will see more superior wind vanes at the top of church spires. These generally have the four compass points on them and again, an arrow points towards the direction the wind is blowing to.

There are a number of ways to measure wind direction. If you know of a wind vane nearby, such as on a church or school, you could just use that for the purpose of your study. You would need to visit this vane daily to take a reading. Alternatively, you could use the internet to find out wind direction in your area.

If you want to make your own wind vane, this can be done relatively simply:

1 Take a drinking straw and cut off the bendy part.
2 Make a slot on both sides using scissors.
3 Cut out a large square from the card and a smaller triangle.
4 Slide the square and triangle into either end of the straw, into the slots that you have already cut. You will need to use sticky tape to stick these into position.
5 Fill your cup with a heavy object or even some stones from your garden to weigh it down.
6 Pierce a hole in the top of the cup's lid, big enough to hold a pencil securely.
7 Ideally, your pencil will have a rubber at the top, stick a pin through the middle of the straw and into the rubber of the pencil to hold it in place.
8 Using a compass, mark on the compass points. You will need to do this at your chosen location.
9 Find a suitable location for your wind vane and secure it. Ideally your wind vane should be on top of a building so that it is in the open air with no obstructions. This may not be possible if you are using a home-made wind vane. In which case, the only thing to consider is that it should be placed away from buildings and trees, in an open space.
10 Try to ensure your wind vane is raised as much above ground as possible.

Things to consider

Your wind vane might not give you very accurate results due to the nature of its construction. Rather than this being a negative, you can discuss this in your assignment (for National 5, this would be in the *Describe and explain, in detail, your main findings* section; for Higher, this would fall under the *evaluation of a research method section*).

How to measure wind speed

Wind speed refers to how fast or slow the wind is blowing.

Equipment required

☞ Anemometer
☞ Or materials to construct an anemometer (five paper cups, drinking straws, pin, hole punch, stapler, pencil with rubber, stopwatch)
☞ Record sheet

Method

Wind speed is measured using an anemometer. There are a number of ways that you could measure wind direction. If you know of an anemometer nearby you could just use that for the purpose of the study. You would need to visit this daily to take a reading. Alternatively, you could use the internet to find out wind speed in your area.

If you want to make your own anemometer, this can be done relatively simply:

1 Make a hole in four of the paper cups using a sharp pencil or scissors. The hole should be about 2 cm from the rim.
2 Take four straws and push them through the holes in the cups, so that about 1 cm is inside the cup. Attach the straw in place using a stapler.
3 In the fifth cup, make four holes around the cup, equally spaced apart.
4 Attach the four cups with straws to the fifth cup; all four paper cups should be facing the same direction.
5 Secure in place as before, using a stapler.
6 The straws will overlap in the centre of the fifth cup; secure them in place using the pin.
7 Make another hole in the bottom of the fifth cup.
8 Poke a pencil through this hole with the rubber side in the middle of the cup.
9 Push the pin into the rubber to hold everything in place.
10 To measure the wind speed, take the anemometer outside, find a suitable location (see below) and using your stopwatch count how many times the anemometer spins round in one minute. It might be helpful to make a red mark on one of the cups so that you can keep count more easily. Ten turns in one minute is equal to 1 mph.
11 You need to find a suitable location for your anemometer. It should be placed away from buildings and trees, in an open space.

If your study does not require actual wind speeds then you could use the Beaufort scale (Table 3.7) to indicate the strength of the winds. The Beaufort scale is a way of measuring wind intensity by looking at visual markers. In the past, the Beaufort scale used sea conditions, but you can use land conditions too.

Table 3.7 Beaufort scale

Beaufort number	Description	Wind speed	Land conditions
0	Calm	1 mph	Smoke rises vertically
1	Light air	1–3 mph	Smoke moves in direction of wind but is not strong enough to move a wind vane
2	Light breeze	4–7 mph	Leaves rustle, wind vanes start to move
3	Gentle breeze	8–12 mph	Leaves and twigs move constantly
4	Moderate breeze	13–18 mph	Small branches move, loose paper might blow about
5	Fresh breeze	19–24 mph	Small trees in leaf begin to sway
6	Strong breeze	25–31mph	Umbrella use becomes difficult; large branches move
7	High wind	32–38 mph	Whole trees in motion; difficulty walking against the wind
8	Gale	39–46 mph	Cars affected by the wind; walking outside is very difficult
9	Strong/severe gale	47–54 mph	Some small trees and temporary signposts may blow over

⇨

Table 3.7 (cont.)

Beaufort number	Description	Wind speed	Land conditions
10	Storm	55–63 mph	Trees can blow over or become uprooted; building damage is likely
11	Violent storm	64–72 mph	Widespread building and structural damage
12	Hurricane force	73+ mph	Severe and widespread damage to buildings and vegetation; debris and unsecured objects are hurled about

Things to consider

Your anemometer might not give you very accurate results due to the nature of its construction. Rather than this being a negative, you can discuss this in your assignment (for National 5, this would be in the *Describe and explain, in detail, your main findings* section; for Higher, this would full under the *evaluation of a research method* section).

Observing cloud amount and type

Cloud amount refers to how much of the sky is occupied by clouds.

Equipment required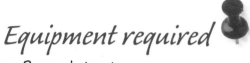
☞ Record sheet

Method

Cloud amount

Clouds are measured in oktas or eighths of the sky (Table 3.8). A sky completely covered in clouds would be described as 8 oktas of cloud cover. If there were no clouds in the sky there would be 0 oktas. This measurement is too detailed for everyday use, however, and is quite difficult to judge. Using five states of sky is sufficient.

Table 3.8 Cloud measurement in oktas

Cloud amount	Description	Estimation of oktas
Clear	No clouds in the sky	0 oktas
Some cloud	Less than half the sky is covered in clouds	2 oktas
A lot of cloud	Half the sky is covered in clouds	4 oktas
Mainly cloudy	More than half the sky is covered in clouds	6 oktas
Complete cloud	All the sky is covered by clouds	8 oktas

Cloud type

Clouds are constantly moving and changing. There are ten main cloud types, as shown in Table 3.9.

Table 3.9 Cloud type

Cloud type		Description	Image
High clouds	Cirrus	Found between 18,000 and 40,000 feet, these are delicate, wispy clouds that look like tufts of hair. During the day, they appear very white while at sunset they may take on the colours of the sunset.	
	Cirrocumulus	Found between 20,000 and 40,000 feet, these clouds are actually lots of small white clouds grouped together. They appear like ripples in the sky.	
	Cirrostratus	Found between 18,000 and 40,000 feet, these are transparent clouds that cover large areas of the sky.	
Medium clouds	Altocumulus	Found between 2,000 and 18,000 feet, these clouds are small patches of cloud. They are mainly found in settled weather. The clouds themselves can appear white or grey and are mainly made up of water droplets.	
	Altostratus	Found between 7,000 and 18,000 feet, these clouds are spread over large areas. They are grey or blue in colour and made up of a mixture of water droplets and ice crystals.	
	Nimbostratus	Found between 2,000 and 10,000 feet, these are layers of cloud. They can be dark grey or bluish grey and they are thick enough to cover the sky and block out the sun. These clouds tend to be accompanied by continuous heavy rain or snow.	

Table 3.9 (cont.)

Cloud type		Description	Image
Low clouds	Stratocumulus	Found between 1,200 and 6,500 feet, these clouds are patchy, varying in colour from bright white to dark grey. These clouds appear in all types of weather.	
	Stratus	Found between 0 and 6,500 feet, these clouds are layers or patches of fuzzy grey clouds. They are very low-level clouds that often appear at ground level.	
	Cumulus	Found between 1,200 and 6,500 feet, these clouds are usually found in fair weather. The tips of these clouds are mainly bright white and darker underneath. They tend to be separate from each other.	
	Cumulonimbus	Found between 1,100 and 6,500 feet, these clouds are thick, dense clouds, better known as thunderclouds. They are generally associated with extreme weather such as torrential rain, hail storms and lightning.	

Drawing weather station circles

Equipment required

☞ Weather information — either collected yourself or from another source

☞ Pencil

Method

Weather station circles are diagrams showing all the weather conditions at a particular time/on a particular day. They are an alternative to writing out the full weather forecast. Each weather element is shown on a weather station circle and has an associated symbol.

Figure 3.4 Cloud cover symbols

Figure 3.5 Precipitation symbols

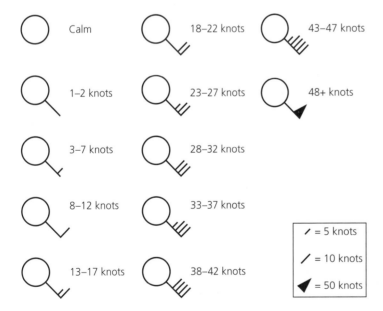

Figure 3.6 Wind speed symbols

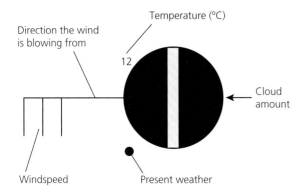

Figure 3.7 Example of a weather station circle

Weather theory

Air masses

Air masses are large bodies of air in which the temperature, humidity and pressure are very similar.

There are five main air masses that affect the UK. Each air mass brings with it the weather from where it originated.

Air masses can develop over oceans (maritime) or over continents (continental).

Arctic Maritime

This air mass develops over the North Pole and the Arctic Ocean and brings very cold, wet weather. In the winter, it usually brings hail and snow. It is uncommon for the Arctic Maritime air mass to affect the UK in summer months, but if it does so, it tends to bring heavy rain and low temperatures.

Polar Maritime

This air mass develops in the North Atlantic Ocean, near Canada and Greenland. This is the most common air mass to affect the UK and it brings wet weather all year round. It can bring strong winds as well.

Polar Continental

This air mass develops over Eastern Europe and Russia and only affects the UK during winter. The Polar Continental brings very cold, dry weather with it, with little wind. Temperatures can remain freezing all day with this air mass.

Tropical Maritime

This air mass develops in the tropical Atlantic Ocean near Bermuda. The air here is warm and moist so the Tropical Maritime brings warm, wet weather in the summer months. In the winter months, it will bring mild, wet weather. There can be quite strong winds with this air mass, generally in a south-westerly direction.

Tropical Continental

This air mass develops over North Africa and the Sahara. The Tropical Continental is most common during the summer months and it brings with it hot, dry weather. It is found in anticyclones (see page 100).

Depressions and synoptic charts

Depressions form when two air masses of conflicting properties meet. The boundary between the two air masses is called a **front**. Warm and cool air do not mix as they have different densities. Instead, the warm air rises and creates an area of low pressure. This area of low pressure is called a depression. Winds in a depression blow anticlockwise towards the low pressure. A depression has a warm front, a warm sector and a cold front.

Cold front

A cold front forms when cold air undercuts warmer air. Cold air is able to do this as it is heavier than warm air. Cold fronts are represented on a synoptic chart as a line of blue triangles.

Warm front

A warm front forms when warm air rises up over cold air. Warm air is lighter than cold air. Warm fronts are represented on a synoptic chart as a line of red semi-circles.

Warm sector

The warm sector is an area of warmer air found in between the warm front and the cold front. When all the warm air in the warm sector has been pushed upwards, the depression dies out.

Occluded front

Occluded fronts form when the cold front catches up with the warm front. The air is pushed up from the surface. Occluded fronts are represented on a synoptic chart as a mixture of triangles and semi-circles.

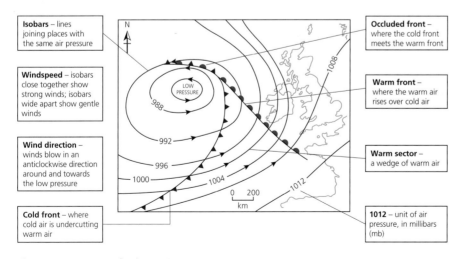

Figure 3.8 Features of a depression

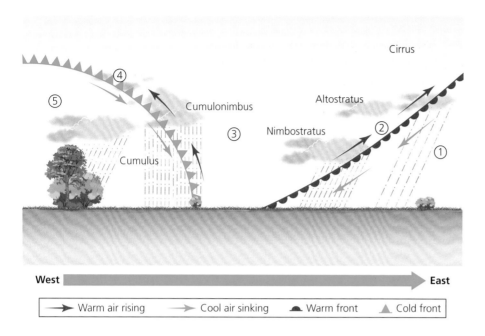

Figure 3.9 Passing of a depression

Table 3.10 Weather at different stages of the depression

Stage	Weather description
Stage 1: Cold air sector	Dry Cold A few high clouds South-east wind Air pressure is falling
Stage 2: Warm front	Steady rain Becoming warmer Lower, thick clouds Air pressure is falling
Stage 3: Warm sector	Drizzle Warm Clear skies South-west wind
Stage 4: Cold front	Heavy rain Becoming cold Large clouds
Stage 5: After the cold front	Rain eases Cold Fewer clouds North-west wind Air pressure is rising

Anticyclones

Anticyclones are areas of high pressure, which occur when the air is sinking.

In an anticyclone:
- winds blow clockwise and outwards
- isobars are widely spaced out, giving light winds
- there is dry weather with few clouds.

The weather brought by anticyclones is different in summer and winter.

Weather in summer:
- Dry
- Light winds/calm
- Sunny, few clouds
- Hot during the day
- Cold at night
- Early morning dew
- Occasional thunderstorms

Weather in winter:
- Dry
- Light winds/calm
- Sunny, few clouds
- Cold during the day
- Frost at night
- Early morning fog

Example National 5 assignment
Processed Information

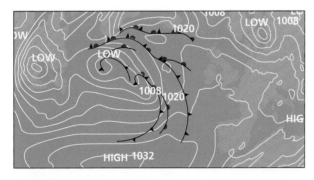 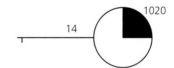

Figure 1 Monday 16 May 2016 (Day 1)

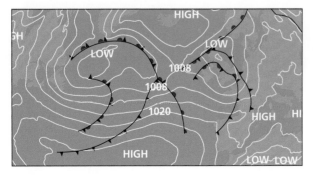 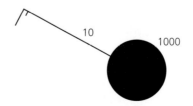

Figure 2 Tuesday 17 May 2016 (Day 2)

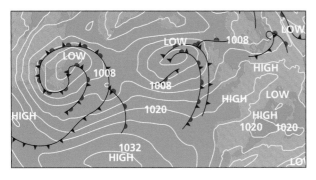
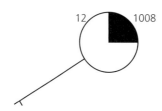

Figure 3 Wednesday 18 May 2016 (Day 3)

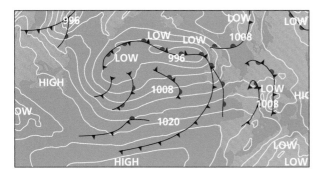
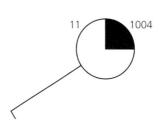

Figure 4 Thursday 19 May 2016 (Day 4)

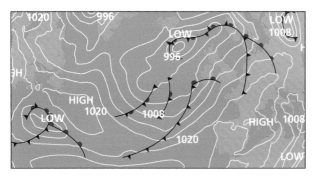
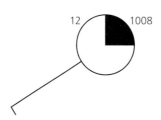

Figure 5 Friday 20 May 2016 (Day 5)

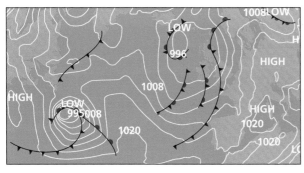
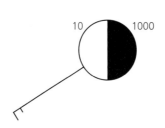

Figure 6 Saturday 21 May 2016 (Day 6)

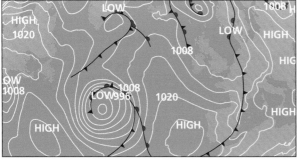
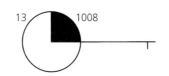

Figure 7 Sunday 22 May 2016 (Day 7)

National 5 Geography assignment	
Candidate name:	Joe Bloggs

State the topic or issue you have researched

The aim of my assignment was to investigate how the weather changes over the course of a week.

Research methods (6 marks)

Describe two research methods you used to collect information about your topic or issue.

1   I measured the weather characteristics

In order to collect first hand data on weather characteristics I had to create a simple weather station in my garden. Here I had the instruments that I needed to collect information on:

- temperature
- precipitation
- wind direction
- wind speed.

To measure the wind speed I constructed my own anemometer. I placed the anemometer on the other side of the garage from the wind vane. Here it was in the open air, away from buildings that may cause obstructions. Every day at 5pm I recorded the wind speed, using the calculation 10 spins = 1 mph.

2   I researched weather information

In order to collect weather information to compare and account for my own findings from my weather station, I used the website www.bbc.co.uk/weather as well as www.metoffice.co.uk. I found the BBC website to be more accessible than the Met Office, however it was useful to compare the two websites. Using these websites I analysed the synoptic charts for each of the seven days of my weather diary, as this would provide the explanation for my results.

Conclusions (14 marks)

For this section you must:

(i) Describe and explain, in detail, the main findings of your research.

(ii) State what conclusions you have reached about your topic or issue.

Description of findings

Figure 1 shows the synoptic chart and weather station circle for Day 1 – Monday 16 May. From the station circle it is clear that the weather on this day was quite settled. The temperature was 14 °C, there was no precipitation, cloud cover was 2 oktas, cloud type was cirrus, the wind direction was westerly and the wind speed was 4 knots.

Figure 2 shows the synoptic chart and weather station circle for Day 2 – Tuesday 17 May. From this station circle the weather was unsettled. The temperature was 10 °C, 17 mm of precipitation was recorded, there was full coverage of thick cloud, with 8 oktas, cloud type was cumulonimbus, the wind direction was north-westerly and the speed was 12 knots.

Figure 3 shows the synoptic chart and weather information for Day 3 – Wednesday 18 May. From studying the weather station circle it is clear that temperatures on this day were 12 °C, there was no precipitation, a light covering of cloud, with 2 oktas, cloud type was cirrus and there was a south-westerly wind measuring 7 knots.

Figure 4 shows the synoptic chart and weather station circle for Day 4 – Thursday 19 May. From this station circle we can see that on this day temperatures were 11 °C, 14 mm of rainfall was recorded, there were 2 oktas of cloud cover, with stratocumulus clouds and the wind direction was south-westerly, measuring 10 knots.

Figure 5 shows the synoptic chart and weather station circle for Day 5 – Friday 20 May. From the station circle we can see that temperatures were 12 °C and 7 mm of rainfall was recorded. There was little cloud cover, only 2 oktas of cirrus cloud recorded. There was a south-westerly wind direction, with a wind speed of 8 knots. ⇨

Figure 6 shows the synoptic chart and weather station circle for Day 6 – Saturday 21 May. By analysing the station circle, it is clear that the weather on this day was quite changeable. Temperatures of 10 °C were recorded and 19 mm of rainfall was measured. The cloud cover was 4 oktas and cloud type appeared to be altocumulus. There was a south-westerly wind direction of 12 knots.

Finally, Figure 7 shows the synoptic chart and weather station circle for Day 7 – Sunday 22 May. The weather here appears very settled. The temperature is 13 °C, there was no precipitation recorded, cloud cover was very light, with 2 oktas observed. The cloud type appeared to be cumulus. There was an easterly wind direction measuring 6 knots.

Explanation of findings

According to my findings, the weather in my local area was quite changeable. There was a mixture of calm, settled weather and a couple of days of more unsteady weather. On Day 1, the weather was very stable, the temperatures were mild, there was no rainfall and there was little wind. By studying the synoptic chart for the same day, it is clear to see why this would be the case. My weather station didn't include a barometer so I was unable to measure air pressure. From the synoptic chart for Monday 16 May, it is evident that my local area (Glasgow) was experiencing high pressure, approximately 1020 mb. High pressure brings dry, settled weather. The distance between the isobars explains why there was so little wind that day as they are very far apart. The direction of the isobars shows the wind direction to be westerly, which is what I recorded using my wind vane.

Day 2 had significantly more unsettled weather. Temperatures were still mild, however there was much more precipitation recorded on this day. Wind speeds were stronger and there was a clear difference in weather conditions from the previous day. Looking at the synoptic chart for Tuesday 17 May, there was a series of weather fronts moving across the UK. The air pressure had dropped to 1000 mb and low pressure was now dominating Glasgow. A cold front passed over Glasgow earlier that day, which helps to explain why such a large volume or rainfall was recorded. An occluded front was moving east over the UK, and when I carried out my measurements at 5pm there was already evidence of its arrival. I recorded thick, cumulonimbus clouds covering all 8 oktas of the sky. The typical weather conditions brought by an occluded front are changeable with heavy rain and thick cloud. Wind speeds will most likely increase as well. Wind speeds were calm when I recorded them at 5pm, which is also evident from the synoptic chart as the isobars were relatively spaced out. However, I anticipated wind speeds increasing when the occluded front was overhead.

The weather on Day 3 was far more settled than the previous day. This is because the weather front that was over my location on Day 2 had now moved west across the UK. According to the synoptic chart, Glasgow was still experiencing low pressure, approximately 1008 mb and a depression was sweeping across the UK. From the synoptic chart it appears that Scotland was affected by a warm front earlier that day, however this must have missed Glasgow as there was no evidence of rainfall at 5pm. At this time, Glasgow appears to be in the warm sector, where conditions are much more settled. In the warm sector there can be some drizzle, however this is not always the case and Glasgow did not experience any precipitation so far that day at all. Temperatures were mild at 12 °C, there was little cloud cover – only 2 oktas – and a south-westerly wind. All of which coincides with the conditions found in the warm sector. As the cold front approaches from the west, conditions will worsen.

On Day 4, Glasgow was still experiencing low pressure, approximately 1004 mb and temperatures remained mild at 11 °C. There were no weather fronts affecting most of Scotland at that moment other than the very north, where a warm front was overhead. Glasgow remained settled with few clouds, only 2 oktas and wind speeds were 10 knots.

The synoptic chart shows a gentle, south-westerly breeze at this time. Glasgow appears to have been affected by the weather fronts that were evident from the previous day's synoptic chart overnight as there was quite a lot of rainfall recorded in my rain gauge at 5pm, although there was no evidence of any precipitation that day. It is evident from the synoptic chart that a depression was moving west towards Scotland.

Day 5 was a reasonably settled day. From the weather station circle it is clear that the weather conditions were fine; 7 mm of rainfall was recorded, which was most likely from the weather front that was identified on the synoptic chart from Day 4. This most likely occurred overnight as there was no evidence on this day of any rainfall. Although Glasgow was still experiencing low pressure, it was higher on Day 5, approximately 1008 mb. Temperatures were mild and there was a gentle, south-westerly wind. The reason for the fine conditions is evident from the synoptic chart as there were no weather fronts affecting Glasgow on Day 5. Despite there being low pressure, conditions were fine and dry as there were no depressions nearby. Isobars were relatively spaced out, accounting for the calm conditions.

Day 6 brought another weather system as low pressure continued over Glasgow. Day 6 was a much darker, gloomier day, although it got brighter as the day went on. Temperatures were mild, around 10 °C, and cloud cover was 4 oktas at 5pm when I recorded the weather characteristics. I measured 19 mm of rainfall in my rain gauge, which is a high volume. The reason for these conditions is clear from the synoptic chart. Despite the weather conditions being settled at 5pm, Glasgow was affected by a weather system that was moving east across the UK. The warm front must have passed over Glasgow earlier that day or overnight, bringing the steady rain associated with warm fronts, followed by a cold front, which appears to have just literally moved over Glasgow. The cold front would have brought short periods of heavy rain. This explains why there is such a lot of rainfall recorded on 21 May.

Finally, Day 7 had considerably more settled weather, brought by the higher air pressure. There was no precipitation recorded that day and the reason is clear from the synoptic chart – there were no weather fronts affecting any of the UK on 22 May. Due to the higher air pressure, temperatures were mild, cloud cover was low, with only 2 oktas recorded and wind speeds were calm at approximately only 6 knots, which again is clear from the lack of isobars over the UK. Overall, this day was a very settled weather day.

Conclusion

The aim of my assignment was to investigate how the weather changes over the course of a week.

The UK has very changeable weather, particularly at this time of year. This is mainly due to the UK being an island which is affected by five different air masses, all of which bring completely different weather conditions. During the course of the week of my study, the UK, but most importantly Glasgow, was affected by predominantly low pressure, which brought the unsettled weather on Days 2, 4, 5 and 6 when weather fronts were over my location. The type of precipitation and weather conditions depends on the type of weather front. On Day 2 a cold front had previously affected Glasgow and it was starting to witness the weather brought by an occluded front, while on Day 6 there was a cold front overhead. Cold fronts bring short periods of heavy rain and occluded fronts bring very unsettled weather, with potentially high levels of precipitation. On the remainder of the days the weather was far more settled although generally still within the low pressure system, other than Day 1, which was high pressure. On Day 1 Glasgow experienced all the weather conditions associated with high pressure: dry conditions, warm temperatures and little cloud.

I carried out my recordings at my weather station at the same time every day – 5pm. However, if I was to carry out this type of investigation again, I would record the weather at two different times of the day, morning and evening, as this would allow me to see exactly how the weather changes throughout the course of the day. I would also record the synoptic charts at the two different times as it is amazing how changeable our weather can be and this would bring more accurate results.

Don't forget – you only have one hour to write up your assignment!

3.4
Coastal study

Choosing a title

Now that you have opted to carry out a coastal study, you must choose an appropriate title. For this, you must decide what aspect of coastal landscapes you want to focus on, for example, are you going to look at a specific coastal landscape in detail? Or are you just going to concentrate on one specific aspect, such as coastal erosion, focusing on corries? There is a lot to think about, so here are some ideas.

Things to consider

1. Are stones found near coastal cliffs larger and more angular than those found at the water's edge?
2. How and why do beach profiles vary along the coast?
3. Are waves more frequent during periods of rain?
4. Does wave frequency affect erosion?
5. Does vegetation change along sand dunes?
6. Do pebbles become smaller and more rounded in the direction of longshore drift?
7. Is there a relationship between the geology of a coastal area and the landforms that are formed there?
8. Is there a relationship between cliff height and slope and the presence of a beach?
9. Are there more scree slopes found in areas of coastal erosion or deposition?
10. Do wave types differ between two coastal areas?

Top tip
Don't make your title too complicated otherwise you will confuse yourself and the marker.

Collecting evidence in the field

In the exam, you need to describe two research methods used to collect information about your chosen topic. However, in practice you will probably have to carry out many more and you can choose two of your 'best' for the exam.

Before you start

Before you start your coastal study there are several things that you have to consider. You will need to do the following:

★ Choose a title.
★ Write down all the research methods you will need to carry out to fully investigate your title.
★ Write down all the equipment you will need.
★ Choose a suitable coastal area and section(s) of coast that you will need to visit. ⇨

⇨
* ★ Choose a suitable day(s) to carry out your investigation. Remember safety is the most important thing so don't carry out this research in an area that is known to be dangerous or on a day when the weather is poor.
* ★ Think about your processing techniques and how you will show the information that you have collected. If you plan to draw field sketches, why not use a camera/camera-phone to take photos that you can use to draw a field sketch from later rather than doing it on the day.

Measuring and recording coastal processes

How to measure wave frequency

Wave frequency is the number of waves that break on the beach.

Equipment required

☞ *Record sheet*
☞ *Pen/pencil*

Method

1 Select a point on the beach or shore.
2 Count the number of waves that break on the beach or pass the point in one minute.
3 If you prefer, you can use a longer period of time, such as five minutes, but you will need to divide the total by the number of minutes to get the number of waves per minute. The following calculation will give you the total number of waves per minute:

$$\text{Waves per minute} = \frac{\text{Total number of waves}}{\text{minutes}}$$

Example: Calculating the number of waves per minute

$$\text{Waves per minute} = \frac{35}{5} = 7 \text{ waves per minute}$$

Things to consider

A frequency of waves under ten is generally considered low, while ten or more is considered high.

How to measure longshore drift

Longshore drift is the movement of sand along a beach.

Equipment required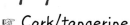

- ☞ Cork/tangerine
- ☞ Tape measure
- ☞ Stopwatch
- ☞ Record sheet
- ☞ Pen/pencil

Method

1. Measure a distance of 10 m across the shore, parallel to the water.
2. Mark your start and end points in the sand.
3. Throw your float into the water making sure you throw it far enough to give you time to get organised in terms of timing.
4. When the float passes the start point, start your stopwatch.
5. Stop timing when the float passes the end point.
6. You can work out the speed of the current using the following calculation:

$$\text{Speed} = \frac{\text{Distance}}{\text{Time}}$$

Example: Measuring longshore drift

$$\text{Speed} = \frac{10\,\text{m}}{75\,\text{seconds}} = \frac{0.13\,\text{m}}{\text{sec}}$$

Things to consider

1. The weather can significantly affect your results, particularly the wind speed and direction. You could take note of this on the day of your study.
2. Obstructions can also affect your result. Either select a distance where there are no obstacles or record these obstacles and explain these fully in your write-up.
3. Always take extra floats, as you will probably lose a few.

How to measure beach profile

A beach profile is a cross-section of a beach; it will show changes in the gradient of the beach from the sea to the shore.

Equipment required

- ☞ Tape measure
- ☞ Clinometer
- ☞ Compass
- ☞ Poles
- ☞ Record sheet
- ☞ Pen/pencil

Method

1 Place one pole at the low tide mark (1) and one at the very far end of the beach (6).
2 Place more poles at points where the slope or angle of the beach changes and mark these as 2, 3, 4, 5.
3 For each change in slope, i.e. at points 1–2, 2–3, 3–4, etc., first measure the distance between each point.
4 Now use a clinometer to work out the angle of the slope from each point.
5 Repeat this process for each of the points.
6 Record this information on the record sheet.

Coastal theory

Waves

Waves are formed by the wind blowing the surface of the sea/ocean or lake. The energy of a wave depends on:
● the strength of the wind
● how long the wind is blowing for
● the depth of the water
● the fetch of a wave (the distance the wave travels in the open water before reaching land).

Constructive and destructive waves

Constructive waves tend to be small waves that appear relatively flat but have a long wave length. These form when there is a long fetch distance. Constructive waves tend to have a low frequency, perhaps only 6–8 waves per minute. They have limited energy but they do have a strong swash that can transport material up a beach. Constructive waves tend to form shallow, longer beaches.

Destructive waves are larger waves that have more height than constructive waves. Destructive waves have a short wave length. They form when there is shorter fetch distance. They tend to have a high frequency, approximately 10–14 waves per minute. Upon approaching a beach, these waves steepen rapidly and then plunge over the beach, creating a powerful backwash. The swash of a destructive wave is weak in comparison.

Wave refraction

The shape of a coastline can alter the direction that an incoming wave is moving in. Waves travel faster in deeper water and slower in shallower water. Water tends to be shallower around the coast. When a wave approaches the coast at an angle, the side nearest the coast, in shallower water, rapidly loses more energy because of friction. This means the wave slows down and changes direction (refracts).

Coastal erosion

Hydraulic action is simply the sheer force of the water/waves hitting against a rock surface, such as a cliff. The force of the water has the ability to dislodge rocks, weakening and changing the rock surface.

Attrition is the breaking up of boulders and rocks in the sea. Rocks knock against each other while being transported by the waves. This wears them down, causing the rock to become smoother and more rounded.

Corrasion is the process where boulders, stones and pebbles are hurled against the cliff edge, breaking down the rock surface.

Solution is where minerals in the rock react with the salt in the seawater, accelerating the break-up of the rock. Solution is a form of chemical weathering.

Features of coastal erosion

Coastlines are affected by erosion but the rate of erosion depends on two factors: the force of the waves and the geology of the coastline.

Headlands are areas of resistant rock that protrude into the sea. **Caves** form when the weaknesses in the rock are attacked by waves. When two caves form on either side of a headland, **arches** may form if they erode back into each other. The roof of an arch might eventually collapse under its own weight, leaving behind a solid piece of rock, now separate from the headland and known as a **stack**. Continued erosion by the waves will mean the stack will collapse, leaving a small lump of rock known as a **stump**.

Wave-cut platforms form on cliffs. Waves attack the base of the cliff, forming a **wave-cut notch**. The notch becomes enlarged over time due to constant wave action. Weaknesses begin to appear in the rock above the notch and run vertically up the cliff. Water that gets pushed up these cracks might explode over the land as a **blowhole**. The many weaknesses running through the cliff and the size of the notch mean that the cliff will eventually collapse, leaving behind a slab of rock at the water surface, known as a wave-cut platform.

Headlands form in areas where the coastline is made up of different rock types. There will be bands of rock running perpendicular to the coastline, made up of hard rock (such as chalk) and soft rock (such as clay). Soft rock is worn down more easily and then the hard, more resistant rock is left protruding into the sea. The areas where the soft rock has been eroded right back are known as **bays**.

Coastal transportation

The sea is also an agent of transportation and it transports material in the same way as rivers. How much material the waves carry depends on their energy. Waves that have a lot of energy will transport heavy rocks and boulders. Waves with little energy will only manage to transport fine materials like silt and clay.

Longshore drift is the movement of material along a beach. When waves break, swash carries material up the beach at the same angle as the wave approached. This is the direction of the prevailing wind. The backwash then returns to the sea, picking up some fine beach material. The backwash does not return in the same direction as the swash but returns directly, generally perpendicular to the coast. Over time, sand and shingle move along a beach in a zigzag, known as longshore drift.

Coastal deposition

Beaches

Beaches are made up of sand, pebbles and shingle that have been deposited by the waves. Beaches form where the deposit of material by waves is greater than its removal by the waves' backwash. Beach material is deposited by the waves' swash, then the backwash returns to sea, depositing more material as it does so. The largest, heaviest particles are deposited first and the finer material last. This means that beaches are graded.

There are different types of beach depending on what types of waves affect them. For example, destructive waves form gently sloping beaches, while constructive waves form a more steeply sloping beach.

Sand dunes

Sand dunes are small mounds or ridges of sand. They form when sand is blown across a beach and trapped by vegetation. Seaweed is deposited at the strandline by waves. This seaweed catches the sand that has been blown inland by winds by saltation and forms an embryo dune. Hardy plants are able to colonise these dunes now, but they need to be able to survive an environment with very little fresh water, strong winds, few nutrients and a high salt content. These pioneer plants are essential in dune formation as they slow winds down and catch more sand, creating a yellow dune.

More plants are able to grow on yellow dunes as the conditions are improved by the pioneer plants. The pioneer plants have died and decayed and added nutrients and humus to the soil. Plants that grow on yellow dunes need to have long roots to reach the water table.

As conditions improve even further, so more superior plants are able to grow. The continuous improvement in conditions means that more superior plants are able to colonise the dunes. Eventually climax vegetation will be able to colonise the oldest dunes (grey dunes) that are found furthest up the beach. These dunes are protected by the younger dunes that have formed in front of them.

Sandspits/sandbars

Sandspits and **sandbars** are extended areas of beach that stretch out into the sea (spit) and often rejoin land (bar). They are formed by the process of longshore drift. When a coastline suddenly changes direction, the process of longshore drift continues along a beach. Instead of the sand being deposited on a beach, it is deposited into the open water. Eventually it builds up above sea level to form an extension to the beach. When a sandspit reaches across and rejoins land, it becomes known as a sandbar. Any water enclosed behind the sandbar is known as a **lagoon**.

Key words

Arch: Formed when waves undercut a cliff and cut right through a cave.

Bay is a small body of water that usually forms behind headlands.

Blowhole: Water pushed up vertical cracks in the cliff which have occurred because of a wave-cut notch.

Cave: Formed when waves attack cliffs with resistant rock along lines of weakness such as faults and joints.

Headland: is an area of resistant rock that juts out into the sea.

Lagoon: Water that has been enclosed by a sandbar.

Longshore drift: Movement of material along a beach.

Sandspit/sandbar: A long, narrow accumulation of sand or shingle with one end still attached to land.

Stack: Erosion causes an arch to widen and eventually the roof of the arch collapses, leaving just a piece of rock standing, known as a stack.

Stump: A stack that has been eroded away to leave a small lump of rock.

Wave-cut notch: Formed when high, steep waves break at the bottom of a cliff, causing it to become undercut. As this process continues the cliff collapses, leaving a slab of rock at the water surface known as a **wave-cut platform**.

Example Higher assignment
Processed Information

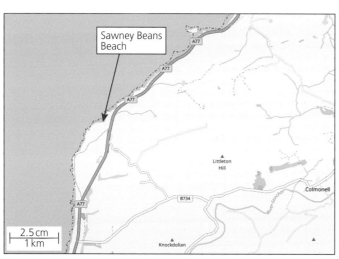

Map 1 OpenStreetMap map showing location of Sawney Beans Beach   **Photograph 1** Cliffs at Sawney Beans Beach

Table 1 Average rock size (water's edge)

Average rock size (cm)	5.2
Average rock shape	Rounded

Table 2 Average rock size (cliff base)

Average rock size (cm)	30.1
Average rock shape	Sub-angular

Table 3 Inter-quartile range of stones found at water's edge and cliff base

	Water's edge	Cliff base
Median	5.25	29.45
Lower quartile	3.4, 3.5, 4.7, 4.9	12.5, 14.7, 17.0, 23.5
Upper quartile	5.8, 6.3, 6.5, 6.7	35.3, 42.5, 47.9, 48.2
Inter-quartile range	2.3	29.35

Table 4 Standard deviation of stone size at water's edge and cliff base

	Water's edge	Cliff base
Standard deviation	1.2	12.6

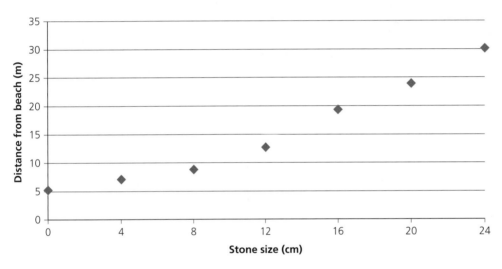

Graph 1 Distance from beach vs stone size

Table 5 Spearman's rank correlation coefficient – distance from beach vs stone size

Site	Distance	Rank distance	Size	Rank size	Difference between ranks	d^2
1	0	7	5.2	7	0	0
2	4	6	7.1	6	0	0
3	8	5	8.8	5	0	0
4	12	4	12.7	4	0	0
5	16	3	19.3	3	0	0
6	20	2	23.9	2	0	0
7	24	1	30.1	1	0	0

$\Sigma d^2 = 0$

Coefficient $(R) = 1 - \dfrac{6\Sigma d^2}{n^3 - n}$

$R = 1 - 0$

$R = 1$

Table 6 Wave frequency

Number of waves in 10 minutes	311
Number of waves per minute	$\dfrac{311}{10} = 31$

Higher Geography assignment	
Candidate name:	Joe Bloggs

Introduction

Knowledge and understanding of the topic.

The aim of my assignment was to investigate if stones found near coastal cliffs are larger and more angular than those found at the water's edge.

I chose to study Sawney Beans Beach, which is a pebble beach on the west coast of Scotland, two miles north of Ballantrae. Before I conducted any investigations I did have an idea about what I would find. From my understanding of wave behaviour, I expected particles to be smallest at the water's edge and increase as you move further away. This is because waves sort the material they are carrying and deposit the particles in order of weight and size. The wave's swash has a lot of energy; therefore, all of the materials are transported up the beach. The largest, heaviest particles are deposited first, at the very back of the beach, as these are the hardest for the wave to continue to transport. As the backwash returns to sea, it gradually loses more and more energy and sediment is then deposited in an ordered way (heaviest/biggest to lightest/smallest) back down to the water's edge.

I also would expect the materials at the back of the beach to be more angular than those found near the water's edge. The reason for this assumption is because the stones found at the water's edge are subjected to far greater wave action than those further up the beach, as most waves break at the shoreline. This means they are subjected to more erosional processes. Waves erode materials in a number of ways. Attrition and corrasion are the two processes that are responsible for shaping the particles. Attrition is the process where the rocks and stones being carried within the waves knock against each other and break each other down. This makes the particles smaller and more rounded. Corrasion is when the rocks and stones are hurled against coastal cliffs breaking them down and again, making them smaller and more rounded.

However, I am aware that other factors can affect particle size. For example, the stones found at the back of the beach may not have been deposited there by waves. They might be the result of freeze-thaw weathering of the coastal cliffs. Any cracks on the rock's cliffs will be subjected to freeze-thaw action where rainwater/seawater enters the cracks. When temperatures drop below zero degrees, the water turns to ice, freezing and expanding, by as much as 9 per cent. This puts a huge amount of pressure on the surrounding rock. When temperatures rise again, the ice melts, releasing that pressure. This is a continuous process and makes the rock very weak. Eventually bits break off and fall to the base of the cliff, where they will shatter, forming various sized particles that will be very angular.

Research methods

A description of the research methods used and/or evaluation of the usefulness and/or reliability of any technique or sources used.

Research method 1: Estimating height of cliff

In order to measure the height of the cliff, I first had to make a clinometer using a protractor and a piece of string. On site, I selected the cliff that I wanted to measure. I chose a safe place to stand from the base of the cliff. There were a lot of large rocks at the foot of this cliff so I had to stand quite far back so that I was on flat land. This meant I was 12 m from the base of the cliff. Using my clinometer I looked along the edge of the protractor to the top of the cliff. I estimated a 1.5 m height from the top of the cliff to account for my height. I recorded the angle on my record sheet. In order to find out the height I completed this calculation:

Height of cliff = Distance (A) × Tan of angle (B) + Height of clinometer from ground

Height of cliff = 12 × Tan (38) + 1.5 = 10.9 m

Research method 2: Measuring stone size and shape

At the water's edge I selected ten stones, chosen at random. I measured each stone's long axis (A axis) using a ruler and I also measured the B and C axes. Using the roundness index I then worked out the shape of the stones. I recorded all of this information on my record sheet. It is worthwhile measuring ten different stones at each site as they may vary and it is good to get an average size and shape. I repeated this at six more locations along the beach so that I could identify any changes taking place.

I also used a measuring tape to work out the distance of each point from the water's edge.

$\Rightarrow$

In future, if I was to conduct a similar study, I would potentially increase the number of stones found at each location. Choosing ten different stones is a reasonable sample, but because so much emphasis was on particle size, it may have been more beneficial to have a sample size of 15–20 stones at each location. This may not affect the results, but because there was such a large range of stone sizes found at the cliff base it might produce more accurate findings. It may also be beneficial to study more than one beach or transect and to take an average in case of a fluke, in order to compare findings. Looking at more than one beach would determine whether these findings were replicated on all beaches like this or whether they were unique to Sawney Beans Beach.

Analysing findings
Using the Processed Information to analyse the information.

Map 1 shows the location of Sawney Beans Beach. The beach itself is situated on the west coast of Scotland, two miles north of Ballantrae. This beach is a good example of a shingle beach and it had steep cliffs at the back and sides of the beach that allowed comparisons of stone size to be made. The cliffs surrounding Sawney Beans Beach are shown in Photograph 1.

Tables 1 and 2 show the average size and shape of the stones found at the water's edge and the cliff base. As expected, the rocks found at the water's edge were smaller and more rounded compared to those found at the base of the cliff. The average stone size at the shoreline was 5.2 cm compared to 30.1 cm found at the cliff base, nearly six times the size. The average shape of stones found at the water's edge was rounded whereas those found at the cliff base were sub-angular.

I wanted to work out the inter-quartile range of the stones found at the two locations to see how varied the size of stones is. At the water's edge the inter-quartile range was 2.3 cm, whereas at the cliff base the range was 29.35 cm. These results are shown in Table 3. I also wanted to work out how far these values are from the average, using standard deviation. Table 4 shows the results of these calculations. At the water's edge the standard deviation was 1.2 cm, whereas at the cliff base the variance was 12.6 cm. This shows the stones are far more mixed in size at the cliff edge than at the water's edge.

Graph 1 shows the relationship between distance from the water's edge and size of stones. It is clear from the graph that there is a relationship between these two variables, because as the distance from the water's edge increases, so too does the size of the particles. This is emphasised in Table 5, where I used Spearman's rank correlation coefficient to work out the relationship. I calculated a perfect positive relationship between these two factors.

Finally, Table 6 shows wave frequency. Over a 10-minute period, I calculated 311 waves breaking over the beach. Dividing this by 10 shows that there were 31 waves per minute.

From the results it is clear that the stones found at the water's edge are considerably smaller than those found at the base of the cliff. Furthermore, the sample of stones selected shows that there was very little variance between stones found at the water's edge compared to those found at the base of the cliff, where there were stones of all sizes found. The reasons why stones found at the water's edge are much smaller than those found further up the beach is due to beach deposition. Waves carry a huge amount of material and as they approach land, the swash of the wave carries the material up the beach. The swash of the wave generally has more power than the backwash. This means that the wave is able to carry material of all different shapes and sizes up the beach but as it does so it loses energy. In order to conserve energy the wave deposits the largest, heaviest material first, at the back of the beach, and the smallest, lightest material last, at the water's edge. Everything in between is graded in terms of size and weight, which is shown in Graph 1 and Table 5, which clearly shows that the size of the particles increases with the distance from the shoreline.

Another reason why the size of the stones are smaller at the water's edge, and the reason for their difference in shape, is due to erosion processes. The stones at the water's edge are under continuous processes of erosion, such as attrition and corrasion. Most waves break at the shoreline and so the stones found here are constantly being attacked. Attrition is when the rocks and stones inside the waves knock against each other, breaking each other down. Corrasion is when the rocks and stones carried by the waves are hurled against cliffs and rocks and break up and wear down. These two processes make the stones increasingly smaller over time but also make them much smoother and more rounded as the sharp, jagged edges are worn down.

⇨

The back of the beach is also affected by erosional processes but not to the same extent as at the shoreline, which receives far more wave action. Stones at the back of the beach are also affected by attrition and corrasion when the waves reach that far up the beach. This is potentially why many of the rocks in the sample found at the back of the beach were sub-angular as opposed to either angular or very angular.

Many of the stones found at the back of the beach are also not necessarily there due to deposition by waves. As was clear from Tables 2 and 3, there was a wide range of stone sizes found at the base of the cliff, many of which would have been deposited by the waves' normal action. However, it is possible that many of the stones in the sample are the result of other processes, such as hydraulic action and freeze-thaw.

The cliffs on either side of Sawney Beans Beach are most likely made of more resistant rock than those on the beach, as these cliffs jut out into the sea forming small headlands, leaving the beach behind as a more sheltered bay. The rocks on these cliffs will be subjected to more powerful waves that will attack the cliffs by hydraulic action. This is when the sheer force of water hitting the cliff causes the rocks to weaken and break down, eventually breaking off. This is likely to happen on either side of the beach as well as on the cliffs at the back of the beach when the tide comes in. Diagram 1 shows that the cliffs surrounding Sawney Beans Beach are reasonably high. I calculated them to be 10.9 m, and they are almost vertical as well as very exposed to the elements. This means that they will be subjected to freeze-thaw weathering. This continuous process weakens the rock and eventually large segments will break off and fall to the base of the cliff. The broken-off rock from freeze-thaw action is likely to account for the variety of sizes of rock found at the cliff base.

Conclusions

Reach a conclusion, supported, by a range of evidence.

The aim of my assignment was to investigate if stones found near coastal cliffs are larger and more angular than those found at the water's edge.

The results that I got during my investigations were as I had anticipated, based on my knowledge of wave action and coastal deposition.

The size of the stones increased moving further in from the water's edge, due to coastal deposition. Beaches tend to be graded as waves sort their material, depositing larger, heavier stones first furthest up the beach and smaller, lighter material last. The stones at the water's edge are also subjected to constant processes of coastal erosion, such as attrition and corrasion, which help to break up the rock further, making them smaller and more rounded.

The rocks found at the back of the beach, nearest the cliffs, are larger as they have been deposited first by the waves' swash but are also the result of rock falls caused by freeze-thaw weathering from the near-vertical cliff behind.

Overall, it is safe to say that the stones found near coastal cliffs are larger and more angular than those found at the water's edge.

Don't forget – you only have 1 hour and 30 minutes to write up your assignment!

3.5
Urban land use study

Choosing a title

Now that you have opted to carry out an urban land use study, you must choose an appropriate title. For this, you must decide what exactly you want to focus on, for example, are you going to compare two land use zones in the city, such as the CBD and inner city? Or might you compare two different inner-city areas? There is a lot to think about, so here are some ideas.

Things to consider

1 Are the land uses found in the CBD the same as those in the inner city?
2 Which area of the city has the most problems with traffic?
3 What traffic control methods are in operation in the CBD and are they effective?
4 Is the inner city a mixture of old industry and housing?
5 Compare two inner-city areas in the same city.
6 Compare housing in the inner city with housing in the suburbs.
7 Why are some areas more popular for families to live in than others?
8 Is there a relationship between house value and the number of schools in an area?
9 Which area of the city is the most pleasant to live?
10 Are the suburbs the most desirable zone of the city to live?

Top tip

Don't make your title too complicated otherwise you will confuse yourself and the marker.

Collecting evidence in the field

In the exam, you need to describe two research methods used to collect information about your chosen topic. However, in practice, you will probably have to carry out many more and you can choose two of your 'best' for the exam.

Before you start

Before you start your urban land use study there are several things to think about.
★ Choose a title.
★ Write down all the research methods you will need to carry out to fully investigate your title.
★ Write down the equipment, if any, you will need.
★ Plan what area(s) you will need to visit.
★ Choose a suitable day(s) to carry out your investigation. Remember safety is the most important consideration, so do not carry out this research in an area that is known to be dangerous or on a day when the weather is poor. ⇨

★ Think about your processing techniques and how you will show the information that you have collected. If you plan on drawing field sketches, why not take a camera/camera-phone and take photos that you can use to draw a field sketch from later rather than doing it on the day.

Urban land use theory

Urban land use zones

Most cities follow a concentric circle model of urban land use zones, where the urban area grows out from the oldest part of the city. In this model, the central business district (CBD) is in the centre, as this is the oldest part of the city. The inner city surrounds this and the suburbs are located on the outskirts of the city, as shown in Figure 3.10.

Central business district (CBD)
- The oldest part of the city
- Mainly shops and offices
- Highest building density
- Little green space

Inner city
- Built in the nineteenth century
- Mainly old factory buildings and old tenement housing
- High building density
- Little green space

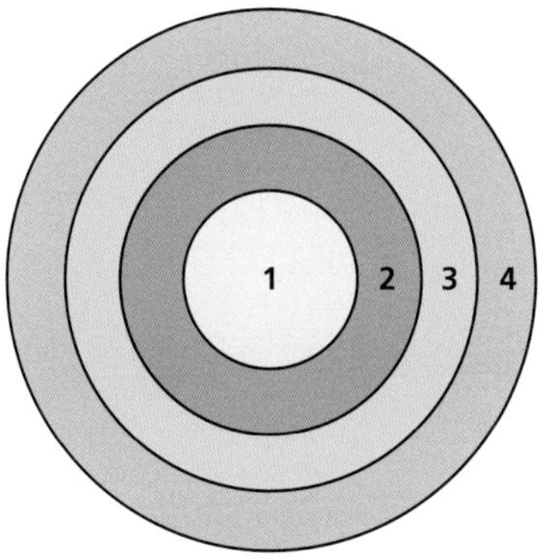

Suburbs
- Built in the twentieth century
- Mainly housing
- Lower building density
- Many parks/areas of green space

Edge of the city
- The newest part of the city, generally dating from the late twentieth century
- Includes out-of-town shopping centres and retail parks
- Lots of greenery
- Low building density

Figure 3.10 Concentric model of urban land use zones

Central business district

There are several features of the CBD that make it easily identifiable:
- highest building density
- many churches – as this is the oldest part of the city
- expensive land
- tall buildings – because land is expensive, buildings are built high rather than long
- high order shops – department stores and specialist shops are found here
- shopping malls and entertainment facilities
- multi-storey car parks
- main business area with offices, banks, company headquarters, etc. – this is because it is the most accessible area of the city
- cultural buildings – town hall, museums, castle, etc.
- area where main roads meet
- location of main bus and train stations

- high pollution levels
- traffic congestion problems – because of the volume of traffic and the grid-iron street pattern

Inner city

- High building density
- Mixture of tenement housing and old factories
- Grid-iron street pattern – narrow streets that were built before motor vehicles were developed
- Tenements built in long straight lines – these were used to house factory workers
- Characterised by old factories, docks and warehouses
- Low order shops
- High pollution levels

Suburbs

- Lower building density
- Mainly housing – semi-detached and detached houses
- Large gardens – because more space available
- A lot of parks and green space – more pleasant environment, which encourages families to settle
- Many schools

Edge of the city

- The newest part of the city, generally dating from the late twentieth century
- Large out-of-town shopping centres
- Retail parks, offices and modern warehouses
- Some housing
- Low building density
- Accessible to main roads and motorways
- A lot of car parking spaces
- Lower land prices

Identifying urban zones using an Ordnance Survey map

Central business district

When looking for the CBD on an Ordnance Survey map, look for:

- railway stations and bus stations
- convergence of main roads
- hotels
- town hall
- lots of churches
- high building density
- grid-iron street pattern.

Inner city

When looking for the inner city on an OS map, look for:

- an inner-city location
- grid-iron street pattern
- chimneys on buildings
- chaotic arrangement of buildings
- large factory buildings
- railways
- rivers or a canal
- high building density
- names such as 'works', 'mill', 'docks' and 'col'.

Edge of the city

When looking for the edge of the city on an OS map, look for:

- an edge-of-town location
- planned arrangement of buildings
- names such as 'industrial estate', 'business park'
- lower building density
- near main roads
- roundabouts.

Example National 5 assignment
Processed Information

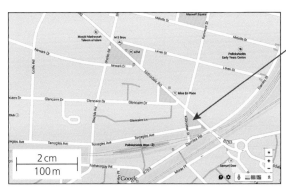

Area of Nithsdale Road being studied

Average house price: 2 bedroom, 1 bathroom flat = £159,000 (January 2016) Source: www.zoopla.co.uk

Map 1 Map of Nithsdale Road by Darnley Road, Glasgow

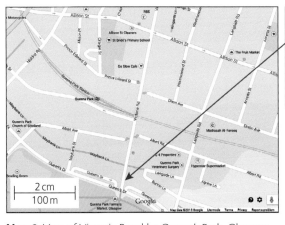

Area of Victoria Road being studied

Average house price: 2 bedroom, 1 bathroom flat = £90,000 (January 2016) Source: www.zoopla.co.uk

Map 2 Map of Victoria Road by Queen's Park, Glasgow

Table 1 Environmental quality survey: Nithsdale Road and Victoria Road

Factor	Nithsdale Road	Victoria Road
Houses with gardens	1	1
Amount of woodland/greenery	3	0
Amount of litter	3	2
Amount of traffic	3	2
Total out of 20	10	5

Table 2 Pedestrian count: Nithsdale Road and Victoria Road

Location	Nithsdale Road	Victoria Road
Date	21 March	22 March
Time	08.30–08.40	08.30–08.40
No. of pedestrians	ЖЖ ЖЖ ЖЖ ЖЖ II	ЖЖ ЖЖ ЖЖ ЖЖ ЖЖ ЖЖ ЖЖ ЖЖ ЖЖ II

Table 3 Vehicle count: Nithsdale Road and Victoria Road

Location	Nithsdale Road	Victoria Road
Date	21 March	22 March
Time	08.45–08.55	08.45–08.55
Lorries	II	ЖЖ ЖЖ II
Buses	IIII	ЖЖ ЖЖ ЖЖ III
Cars	ЖЖ ЖЖ ЖЖ ЖЖ ЖЖ I	ЖЖ ЖЖ ЖЖ ЖЖ ЖЖ ЖЖ ЖЖ ЖЖ ЖЖ ЖЖ ЖЖ ЖЖ ЖЖ ЖЖ
Motorbikes	I	IIII
Vans	ЖЖ	ЖЖ ЖЖ ЖЖ III

Table 4 Land use survey

Nithsdale Road

					RT				
CO	CH	CF	EC	EC	CM	ER	CP	CT	CO

Victoria Road

					RT				
CP	CS	EC	CS	CN	CT	EB	CC	CC	CJ

R	Residential
I	Industrial
C	Commercial
E	Entertainment
P	Public buildings
O	Open space
T	Transport
S	Services

Chart 1 How long have you travelled to use the services on:

Key
- Under 10 minutes
- 10–30 minutes
- 30–60 minutes
- More than 60 minutes

Key
- Under 10 minutes
- 10–30 minutes
- 30–60 minutes
- More than 60 minutes

Nithsdale Road   Victoria Road

Chapter 3.5 Urban land use study

Chart 2 How often do you use the shops and services on:

Nithsdale Road   Victoria Road

National 5 Geography assignment	
Candidate name:	Joe Bloggs

State the topic or issue you have researched

The aim of my assignment was to compare two inner-city areas in Glasgow.

Research methods (6 marks)

Describe two research methods you used to collect information about your topic or issue.

Location

I chose to study two inner-city areas within the catchment area of my school. These are areas that I know well and I am familiar with. Having them close by meant that I could carry out my research easily. The first location I chose was Nithsdale Road in the postal code of G41, which includes Pollokshields and Shawlands. The second location was Victoria Road in the neighbouring postal code of G42, which includes Battlefield, Govanhill, Mount Florida and Strathbungo East.

1 I carried out an environmental quality survey

Before I began the survey I decided what factors would be important to consider when comparing these two areas. I chose to include:

● houses with gardens

● amount of woodland/greenery

● amount of litter

● amount of traffic.

By focusing on these four factors, I felt I should get a good idea of the environmental quality in that area. I decided to carry out my environmental quality survey during rush hour during the week. I carried out the survey on Nithsdale Road on one day (21 March) and the same survey on Victoria Road the following day (22 March). Both surveys were carried out at exactly the same time on consecutive weekdays. I constructed a table showing the four factors and I gave each factor a score of between 0 and 5, with 0 being the worst and 5 being the best.

Scoring houses with gardens was as straightforward as it sounds. Houses/flats that had private gardens were given a higher score than those that either had no garden or had a portion of a communal area. When scoring the amount of woodland and greenery, I only accepted greenery that was actually in the section of the streets that were being studied. At the top of Victoria Road is Queen's Park; however, as this was outside the section being studied it was not taken into account. The amount of litter was based on observations. Areas that had no problems of litter on the streets and plenty of bins were given a score out a 5, while those areas that had rubbish on the streets and few public bins were given 0.

After awarding a score for each of the factors, I was able to give both areas a score out of 20. These results can then be compared. ⇨

2 I designed a questionnaire

Before I began there were several things that I had to consider. First of all, I needed to think about what the purpose of the questionnaire was – what exactly I wanted to get out of it. I decided that the main focus of my questionnaire would be on the shops and services in the two areas and what the catchment area is for them. I produced a questionnaire that was easy to understand and only involved the member of public to tick a box that was relevant to them. This meant the questionnaire was quick and straightforward but gave me all the information that I required. I decided to carry out the questionnaire after rush hour as many people would be rushing trying to get to work and would not want to be inconvenienced. By waiting till after 9am I also found people who were using the shops and services and not people walking past on their way elsewhere.

I made the decision beforehand to approach every 10th person or so and include all ages, sexes, etc. When I approached someone I was polite and explained the purpose of the questionnaire. Then it was up to the person to fill out the form. I found that most people wanted me to tick the boxes for them.

Because I needed to carry out questionnaires at two separate locations I decided to carry out one day and the other the next. I conducted my questionnaire on Nithsdale Road on 21 March at 10.30am and Victoria Road on 22 March at 10.30am.

When I had all the information that I required I was able to put my results into graph form, to make it easier to interpret. I decided to use a pie chart to show the information, as it was relatively straightforward to convert my findings into percentages based on the number of people that I asked.

Conclusions (14 marks)

For this section you must:

(i) Describe and explain, in detail, the main findings of your research.

(ii) State what conclusions you have reached about your topic or issue.

Description of findings

According to the theory of urban land use zones, the inner city is made up of a mixture of old industry and tenement housing. The inner city is generally considered a poorer area of the city that is less desirable to live in than the suburbs. The aim of this study was to show that not all inner-city areas are the same and it is wrong to categorise them in that way.

Map 1 shows the location of the first area being studied, which is Nithsdale Road on the south side of Glasgow. According to www.zoopla.co.uk, the average cost of a two bedroom house on this street is £159,000. Map 2 shows the location of the second area being studied: Victoria Road. This is also on the south side of Glasgow and is in fact a neighbouring area of Nithsdale Road. Here house prices are considerably less, at only £90,000 for the same size of property.

Table 1 shows the results of the environmental quality survey conducted in both areas. Nithsdale Road scored higher with 10/20, while Victoria Road only scored 5/20.

Table 2 shows the volume of pedestrians during the mid-week rush hour. The count had to be carried out at the same time on consecutive weekdays in order to compare the findings. Victoria Road appears to be a far busier street in terms of pedestrians, as I counted 47 between 08.30 and 08.40am, compared to only 22 on Nithsdale Road.

Similarly, Table 3 shows the volume of traffic. I decided to carry out a detailed traffic count so that I could identify the types and volume of vehicles using these two roads. Again, the study was carried out on two consecutive week day mornings between 08.45 and 08.55am. Results were similar in that Victoria Road had a far higher volume of traffic of all types during this time compared to Nithsdale Road. In particular, there were far more cars: 65 on Victoria Road compared to 26 on Nithsdale Road and 18 buses compared to only 4 on Nithsdale Road.

Comparing the land use surveys in Table 4 for Nithsdale Road and Victoria Road it is clear that both streets have the same layout, in terms of shops and services on ground level and tenement housing above. Using the RICEPOTS system of classification it was easy to determine the land use classifications for each of the individual units. Nithsdale Road had some higher order services than Victoria Road, such as florists, hairdressers, cafés and restaurants, while Victoria Road had mainly takeaway food outlets, newsagents and charity shops.

Finally, the pie charts show the results of the questionnaire that I conducted. It is clear from Chart 1 that there is a reasonable difference between the distance that people are willing to travel to use the shops and services on Nithsdale Road compared to Victoria Road. Almost half the shoppers using the services on Victoria Road travel less than 10 minutes to use them, whereas more than half the people using the shops and services on Nithsdale Road had travelled 10–30 minutes to use these services.

When I asked how often the shoppers use these shops and services, the results were quite varied. Very few people used the shops and services on Nithsdale Road every day or even once or twice a week. Most people tended to use these shops on a more irregular basis – either once a week or less, whereas most people using the shops and services on Victoria Road used them either every day or a few times a week. Very few people used them less regularly than that.

Explanation of findings

Both of these areas fall into the same category in terms of urban land use zone, which is the inner city. This is clear from Maps 1 and 2. It is, then, not surprising that the main housing type in both areas is tenement flats. This is typical of an old industrial area. The tenement buildings on both Victoria Road and Nithsdale Road were built during the nineteenth century when Glasgow was industrialising and was involved with many heavy industries such as coal mining and shipbuilding. Over the years, Nithsdale Road has become a more affluent part of the inner city compared to Victoria Road. All of the evidence that was collected emphasises this point.

The land use surveys show the difference in shops and services found on the two streets. The shops and services found on Nithsdale Road tend to be more middle-order shops such as florists, hairdressers and restaurants. These types of shops and services are not used every day, which is highlighted in Chart 2, and people are generally prepared to travel longer distances to use them, which is shown in Chart 1. In contrast, the low-order shops such as the newsagents and takeaway food outlets and services were found on Victoria Road,. Not only are the shops and services found on Nithsdale Road higher order but they are also more affluent types of shops. There were no charity shops found on this section of Nithsdale Road but there were a few found on Victoria Road. Likewise, there were no restaurants found on Victoria Road, but there were a few on Nithsdale Road.

In terms of environmental quality, Nithsdale Road scored considerably better than Victoria Road. Nithsdale Road is cleaner, quieter and leafier than Victoria Road, which makes it a more desirable area to live. Both areas scored low marks for category 'houses with gardens', as the type of residential properties found in both locations were tenement buildings. These do not have private gardens but instead have shared, communal areas where the number of people using the space is dependent on the number of flats in the block. This is typical of tenement housing.

Both Table 2 and Table 3 show that there is a higher volume of both pedestrians and vehicles on Victoria Road during mid-week rush hour. This could be for a number of reasons. Firstly, Victoria Road is a main road and many buses are routed along it, so it is a popular place for passengers to catch connections. This accounts for the difference between 18 buses on Victoria Road and 4 on Nithsdale Road. This study only looked at a section of Victoria Road, but if I were to consider the entire street, it would become clear that there are many shops and services found all the way down Victoria Road, so this would account for the extra people and lorries making deliveries. Beyond this section of Nithsdale Road, it is mainly residential. It is not a main road like Victoria Road, where lots of public transport is routed. Presumably there are more cars than other vehicles using this road, as these are people driving to work.

It is for all of these reasons that Nithsdale Road has far higher property values than Victoria Road.

Conclusion

The aim of my assignment was to compare two inner-city areas in Glasgow.

I found that despite these two areas being located next to each other, the difference in wealth was quite clear. The two areas shared many similarities: they are both 'typical' inner-city locations, they have high building densities, grid-iron street patterns and red sandstone tenement buildings. However, where they differ is the quality of the environment, the type of shops and services found in each area and the volume of traffic, which ultimately affects property prices.

As I was conducting this research on my own, it was impossible for me to carry out the research in two different areas at the same time, which is why I chose two consecutive weekdays. It might be that the results are skewed because of that. Potentially on the day when I was visiting Victoria Road, there was a higher volume of traffic than usual or more pedestrians that might have affected the results. As I cannot be in two places at the same time, the only option to make the results more reliable would be to carry out the same research the following week, this time going to Victoria Road on the Monday and Nithsdale Road on the Tuesday. I could then average the figures in order to make them more accurate.

Only a very small section of Victoria Road and Nithsdale Road were surveyed and it might have been beneficial for my study to increase the area, as this would have taken more factors into account.

As I knew these areas well, I was not surprised by the results I got and I am pleased that my study can show that two inner-city areas can be completely different in terms of affluence, as this shows they cannot all be categorised in the same way.

Don't forget – you only have one hour to write up your assignment!

3.6
Services and settlements study

Choosing a title

Now that you have opted to carry out a study on services found in urban areas, you must choose an appropriate title. For this, you must decide what exactly you want to focus your study on. For example, are you going to look at the different services found in one area of the city or compare two different areas? There is a lot to think about, so here are some ideas.

Things to consider

1 Does the CBD have the most variety of shops and services?
2 Is there a relationship between the size of a settlement and the variety of services found there?
3 Do low-order shops have a smaller catchment area than high-order shops?
4 Explain the distribution of charity shops in the inner city of Glasgow.
5 Compare shopping quality between the CBD and out-of-town shopping centres.
6 What factors affect shoppers choosing the CBD over out-of-town shopping centres or vice versa?
7 Are certain types of shops found in clusters and why?
8 Is there a pattern to the distribution of entertainment facilities in Glasgow's CBD?
9 Compare the entertainment facilities found in two urban areas.
10 Plot the distribution of department stores across an urban transect and explain the findings.

Top tip

Don't make your title too complicated otherwise you will confuse yourself and the marker.

Collecting evidence in the field

In the exam, you need to describe two research methods used to collect information about your chosen topic. However, in practice you will probably have to carry out many more and you can choose two of your 'best' for the exam.

Before you start

Before you start your services and settlements study there are several things to think about.

★ Choose a title.
★ Write down all the research methods you will need to carry out to fully investigate your title.
★ Write down the equipment, if any, you will need.

★ Plan what area(s) you will need to visit.
★ Choose a suitable day(s) to carry out your investigation. Remember safety is the most important thing so don't carry out this research in an area that is known to be dangerous or on a day when the weather is poor.
★ Think about your processing techniques and how you will show the information that you have collected. If you plan on drawing field sketches, why not take a camera/camera-phone and take photos that you can use to draw a field sketch from later rather than doing it on the day.

Services and settlements theory

Settlements

A settlement is simply an area where people settle down to live. Settlements vary in size and are found in a variety of locations. Generally, settlements are categorised according to their size.

The four main settlement types, in order of size, are:

1 hamlet
2 village
3 town
4 city.

A city that has over 10 million inhabitants is classed as a mega city.

Services

The number of services found in a settlement will depend on its size and distance from other settlements of a similar size. Figure 3.11 shows the relationship between a settlement size and its services.

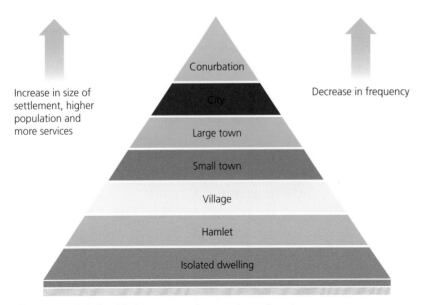

Figure 3.11 Relationship between settlement size and services

Services can be sorted into three main categories: low-order, middle-order and high-order, as shown in Table 3.11. In general, the larger the settlement the greater the variety of services found there.

Table 3.11 Services and settlements

Service category	Type of settlement where found	Example
Low-order services	Village, town, city	Newsagent, post office, bus stop, primary school
Middle-order services	Town, city	Pharmacy, hairdressers, high school
High-order services	City	Department store, chain store, university

Sphere of influence

The reason why some settlements have more low-order shops than larger settlements is to do with a shop or service's sphere of influence. The sphere of influence is the distance which customers are prepared to travel to use that shop or service.

Shops and services such as newsagents and post offices found in small settlements like villages have a small sphere of influence. People are not prepared to travel very far to use these types of services, perhaps only one or two miles.

Towns and cities have a much larger sphere of influence because people are prepared to travel long distances in order to use the shops and services found there. Because the facilities found in towns and cities are high-order shops, people are prepared to travel long distances in order to use them. IKEA in Glasgow had customers travelling from as far as Northern Ireland to buy its products (until a Belfast branch opened in 2007). Cities such as London and New York have global spheres of influence. People travel from all over the world to visit the shops and services there.

However, there are other factors that affect a service's sphere of influence, including:
- place of work
- location of friends
- parking restrictions
- public transport routes
- reputation
- media advertisement
- convenience.

Example Higher assignment
Processed Information

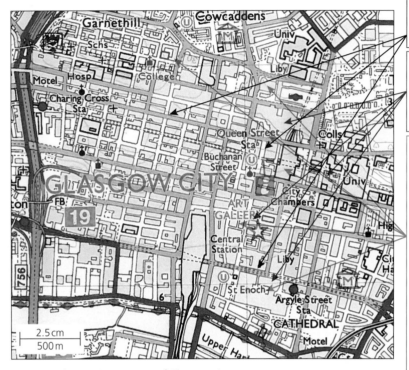

Glasgow CBD's main shopping streets:
- Sauchiehall Street
- Argyle Street
- Buchanan Street

Shopping malls in Glasgow's CBD:

Italian Centre
Buchanan Galleries
St Enoch Centre
Princes Square

Parking:

Buchanan Galleries 2–3 hrs: £4.50
Mon–Sat 7.30–23.30 Sun 9–23.30
Total spaces: 2000

City Parking Cambridge Street, 2–3 hrs: £6.00
Open 24 hrs, 7 days/week
Total spaces: 598

St Enoch Centre, 2–3 hrs: £5
Mon–Wed 7.30–20.00, Thurs 7.30–21.00,
Fri/Sat 7.30–20.00, Sun 8.00–19.00
Total spaces: 900

NCP Mitchell Street, 2–3 hrs: £11.50
Open 24 hrs, 7 days/week
Total spaces: 184, 2 disabled spaces

Glasshouse Car Park, 2–3 hrs: £9.50
Open, 24 hrs, 7 days/week
Total spaces: 515

2.5 cm / 500 m

Map 1 Ordnance Survey map of Glasgow city centre

Braehead is a covered shopping mall with over 110 shops

Braehead has 6,500 free car parking spaces within three different car parks

2.5 cm / 500 m

Map 2 Ordnance Survey map of Renfrew showing Braehead shopping mall

Map extracts reproduced by permission © Crown copyright 2017 Ordnance Survey 100047450.

Table 1 Shopping quality survey: Braehead

Shopping environment quality						
Lower quality	1	2	3	4	5	Higher quality
Few shoppers				✓		Many shoppers
Badly maintained shops – run down					✓	Well-maintained shops
Difficult to access					✓	Easily accessible
Expensive parking					✓	Free parking
Short opening times in car parks					✓	24-hour parking
No pedestrian areas					✓	Fully pedestrianised
Total: 29/30						
Shopping quality						
Lower quality	1	2	3	4	5	Higher quality
Short opening hours				✓		Longer opening hours
Little variety of shops			✓			Large variety of shops
Mainly cheap, low budget shops			✓			Mainly expensive, designer shops
No cafés, bars or restaurants				✓		Many cafés, bars and restaurants
No other entertainment facilities			✓			Many other entertainment facilities
No covered shopping malls					✓	Fully covered shopping malls
Total: 22/30						

Table 2 Shopping quality survey: CBD

Shopping environment quality						
Lower quality	1	2	3	4	5	Higher quality
Few shoppers				✓		Many shoppers
Badly maintained shops – run down				✓		Well-maintained shops
Difficult to access			✓			Easily accessible
Expensive parking	✓					Free parking
Short opening times in car parks			✓			24-hour parking
No pedestrian areas			✓			Fully pedestrianised
Total: 18/30						
Shopping quality						
Lower quality	1	2	3	4	5	Higher quality
Short opening hours				✓		Longer opening hours
Little variety of shops					✓	Large variety of shops
Mainly cheap, low budget shops				✓		Mainly expensive, designer shops
Shopping quality						
Lower quality	1	2	3	4	5	Higher quality
No cafés, bars or restaurants					✓	Many cafés, bars and restaurants
No other entertainment facilities					✓	Many other entertainment facilities
No covered shopping malls			✓			Fully covered shopping malls
Total: 26/30						

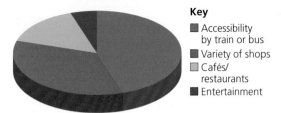

Chart 1 Reasons for choosing Glasgow's CBD over Braehead

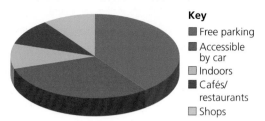

Chart 2 Reasons for choosing Braehead over Glasgow's CBD

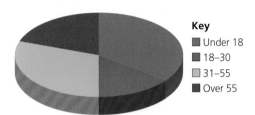

Chart 3 Age group of shoppers using CBD

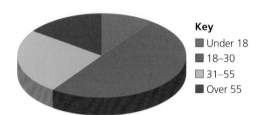

Chart 4 Age group of shoppers using Braehead

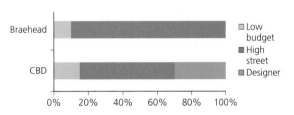

Bar chart 1 Percentage of shops in Braehead and CBD

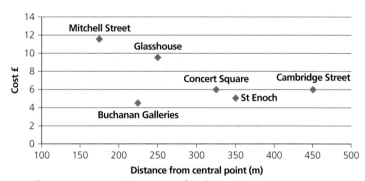

Graph 1 Proximity to CBD vs cost of parking

Table 3 Spearman's rank correlation coefficient

Car park	Distance from central point (m)	Rank distance	Cost of parking (2–3 hrs, £)	Rank price	Difference between ranks	d^2
NCP Mitchell Street	175	6	11.50	1	5	25
St Enoch	350	2	5.00	5	−3	9
NCP Glasshouse	250	4	9.50	2	2	4
Cambridge Street	450	1	6.00	3.5	−2.5	6.25
Buchanan Galleries	225	5	4.50	6	−1	1
Concert Square	325	3	6.00	3.5	−0.5	0.25
$\sum d^2 = 45.5$						
$(R) = 1 - \dfrac{6\sum d^2}{n^3 - n}$						
$(R) = -0.3$						

Higher Geography assignment	
Candidate name:	Joe Bloggs

Introduction
Knowledge and understanding of the topic.
The aim of my assignment was to compare out-of-town shopping centres with the central business district (CBD).
In order to investigate this I have chosen to study Glasgow's CBD, which includes popular shopping areas such as Sauchiehall Street, Buchanan Street and Argyll Street as well as covered shopping malls such as Buchanan Galleries, the Italian Centre and St Enoch Centre. The out-of-town location I have chosen is Braehead, which is a large shopping centre in Renfrewshire, situated off the M8 motorway. ⇨

The number of out-of-town shopping centres has been increasing over recent years and they have become very popular with shoppers. The CBD has seen a marked decline in the number of customers choosing to shop there and many town/city centres have seen the closure of independent and high-street stores.

Out-of-town shopping centres are becoming increasingly popular because they offer several perks over the CBD, such as free parking. Parking in the CBD can be very expensive and it is often quite limited, so free parking and large car parking areas are very appealing. Out-of-town shopping centres are also very accessible by car, which makes them attractive to many shoppers, while city-centre driving can often be busy and frustrating, which is off-putting. Many people visiting out-of-town shopping centres do so because they like that all the shops are in the one area and they can park, shop and eat in restaurants all in the same place. However, shopping in the CBD has a much wider variety of shops as well as cafés, restaurants and entertainment so it remains an important shopping district that is favoured by many.

Research methods

A description of the research methods used and/or evaluation of the usefulness and/or reliability of any technique or sources used.

Glasgow has many out-of-town shopping centres, such as the Fort, the Forge, Silverburn and Braehead. I decided to carry out my investigation using Braehead Shopping Centre (intu Braehead as it is now known) and the central business district of Glasgow.

Research method 1: Land use survey

In order to gather information on the types of shops found at these two locations, I had to visit each one. The shopping areas in Glasgow CBD are concentrated on three main streets: Sauchiehall Street, Buchanan Street and Argyle Street, and in four main shopping malls: Buchanan Galleries, St Enoch Centre, Princes Square and the Italian Centre. I drew a table in order to record the types of shops found on these streets using the following categories:

- charity/low-budget shops
- independent shops
- high-street shops
- designer shops.
- leisure and entertainment facilities

By recording land use over a number of streets, it meant I should have a full picture and avoid having only a snapshot of each location.

As I walked along each street I recorded the number of different shops in each category by using tally marks. I repeated this method at Braehead. I also recorded pedestrianised areas on a base map of the area.

I used Braehead's website to help back up my survey to ensure I had recorded everything correctly.

By using the headings above, my results are limited only to these categories. In future, it might be more useful to record more specifically different types of shops such as clothing, or tech shops, and also be more specific about the entertainment facilities at each point.

It can also be difficult at times to work out what each unit is being used for from outside, particularly services which are not on the ground floor of buildings.

Research Method 2: Shopping quality survey

Before I began the survey I decided what factors would be important to consider when comparing these two areas. I thought it was important to divide my survey into two parts: the first concentrating on the shopping environment and the other on the shops and services. For the shopping environment, I focused on:

- number of shoppers
- how well maintained the shops/shopping centres were
- accessibility
- cost of parking
- car park opening hours
- pedestrianised areas.

The factors I believed were important when assessing shopping quality were:

- opening hours
- variety of shops
- type of shops
- number of cafés/restaurants nearby
- entertainment facilities
- indoor/outdoor shopping areas

By focusing on all of these factors, I should get a very good idea of the overall shopping quality in each area. I decided to carry out my survey on two consecutive Saturdays at the same time. Glasgow CBD was Saturday 20th February and Braehead was Saturday 27th February, both from midday onwards. I drew a table showing each of the factors and gave each a score between 0 and 5, 0 being the worst and 5 the best.

After awarding a score for each of the factors, I was able to give both areas a score for the shopping environment and the shopping quality. These results can then be compared.

Analysing findings

Using the Processed Information to analyse the information.

Location

Maps 1 and 2 show the locations of the two shopping areas. Map 1 is Glasgow Central Business District. From the map it is clear that this is a central location within the city. There is a high building density, showing that the area is very built-up. There are a number of narrow streets running through the area, running at 90° angles to each other to form a grid-iron street pattern. This type of street pattern can lead to traffic problems in the CBD, particularly problems with congestion and pollution.

The main shopping streets have been annotated as well as the four main shopping malls. By annotating this map it is clear that the shops within this shopping district are relatively spread out. By using the scale of the map it is possible to work out that by walking from where Cambridge Street meets Sauchiehall Street to the St Enoch Centre on Argyle Street you cover a distance of over 800 m. It is also clear from Map 1 that this area is accessible by both car and public transport. There are a number of car parks located within the city centre that have been annotated as well as a number of bus and train stations, such as Buchanan bus station and Queen Street and Central train stations. There is also an option of travelling to the CBD by underground and there are three underground stations evident: Buchanan Street, Cowcaddens and St Enoch. All of these make Glasgow's CBD very accessible.

Map 2 shows the location of Braehead shopping centre. From this map it is clear that Braehead has an out-of-town location. The building density is much lower and there is plenty of flat, unused land surrounding it. Again, this is typical of an out-of-town location. The scale of Braehead is obvious from the map; the building is very large, covering almost 500m. There are many main roads that run by Braehead such as the M8 and the A8, both of which make access to Braehead by car straightforward. Map 2 has been annotated to show that there is an abundance of free parking at Braehead, with over 6,500 spaces in three different car parks.

Shopping quality

From the two shopping surveys (Tables 1 and 2) it is clear that in terms of the shopping environment, Braehead has the edge, scoring 29/30 compared to 18/30 for the CBD. The main factor that lets the CBD down here is the problem of parking. Although there are a number of car parks located within the CBD, the cost of these is very high, especially compared to the free parking found at Braehead. In terms of shopping quality, however, the CBD scores highest with 26/30 compared to 22/30 at Braehead. One of the most important factors here is the different variety of shops found in the CBD. As Bar chart 1 shows, the CBD has a wide variety of shops, ranging from the low-budget shops that are found on Sauchiehall Street to the expensive designer shops found in the Italian Centre. Braehead, on the other hand, has mainly high-street stores.

Factors

The pie charts show the questionnaire responses to questions that were asked of shoppers in both the CBD and Braehead. Both sets of shoppers were asked the same questions. First of all, I wanted to find out the age categories of people using the two shopping areas. Charts 3 and 4 show this information. It is clear that there is a relatively even mix of age groups using the CBD, whereas it tends to be people within the 18–30 age group using Braehead. There are a number of reasons why this might be the case. First of all, what is interesting is that there is a high percentage of people in the 31–55 and over 55 age range using the CBD. This could be because this age group tends to have more disposable income and therefore, they might want to make use of the more expensive shops that are found here. There is also quite a high number of under 18s, particularly in comparison to Braehead. This could be a result of Braehead not being very accessible by public transport compared to the CBD. Where the CBD has many underground stations, train stations and bus stations, Braehead has no access to its shopping centre by underground or train and therefore the only way of getting there is by car or bus.

Charts 1 and 2 show what the shoppers considered to be the most important factor when choosing to where shop did. Accessibility by train or bus came out top in the CBD while the free parking was the most attractive feature of the out-of-town shopping centre. The CBD is accessible by car, however, the cost of parking there is very expensive, ranging from £4.50 to £11.50 for 2–3 hours. Graph 1 shows the relationship between cost of parking and the proximity to the CBD. All car parks are located within the CBD, but the distance was worked out from a central point on Buchanan Street that is roughly in the very centre. By using Spearman's rank correlation coefficient, shown in Table 3, it is clear that there is not necessarily a relationship between closeness to the centre and the cost of parking. Car parks appear to charge whatever they wish, although NCP Mitchell Street is the closest and the most expensive car park in Glasgow's CBD. The free parking found at Braehead will be a very appealing alternative.

Conclusions

Reach a conclusion, supported by a range of evidence.

The aim of my assignment was to compare out-of-town shopping centres with the CBD.

Before I began my investigation I had an idea of what results I would get, based on my knowledge of these urban zones and shopping areas. However, what surprised me the most was the shopping quality survey. I thought that both shopping areas would have been relatively even in terms of both environment and quality. I was surprised that the CBD scored so low on the shopping environment. Clearly the main factor that let it down was the cost of parking. This factor continued to appear throughout the study, which is certainly why Braehead has the upper hand when it comes to parking, with 6,500 spaces of free parking.

The CBD and out-of-town shopping centres both appear to have their uses and customers prefer one to the other for completely different reasons. The CBD has a much larger variety of shops to Braehead, making it more attractive to all age groups, although the shops in Braehead cater for the age group that uses it most.

Overall, it is fair to say that there are many differences between shopping in the CBD compared to shopping in out-of-town shopping centres and this is down to a number of factors, although accessibility and parking are two of the most important.

Don't forget – you only have 1 hour and 30 minutes to write up your assignment!

3.7
Tourism study

Choosing a title

Now that you have opted to carry out a tourism study, you must choose an appropriate title. For this, you must decide what exactly you want to focus on, for example, are you going to study one particular tourist town or compare two? Are you going to focus your investigation on the types of services found in tourist centres and how these are distributed? Or might you look at how tourism is managed? There is a lot to think about, so here are some ideas.

Things to consider

1 Compare the similarities and differences between two tourist towns.
2 Are tourist attractions/facilities clustered in one area or spread out?
3 Study the distribution of gift shops in a tourist town.
4 Is there a relationship between the number of tourist facilities and the size of a settlement?
5 Why do tourist attractions differ in popularity?
6 What are the causes and effects of honeypot sites?
7 What are the benefits of tourism on a local area?
8 What are the impacts of tourism on an area?
9 How do National Parks manage tourism?
10 What strategies can be adopted to minimise negative impacts of tourism?

Top tip

Don't make your title too complicated otherwise you will confuse yourself and the marker.

Collecting evidence in the field

In the exam, you need to describe two research methods used to collect information about your chosen topic. However, in practice you will probably have to carry out many more and you can choose two of your 'best' for the exam.

Before you start

Before you start your tourism study there are several things to think about.

★ Choose a title.
★ Write down all the research methods you will need to carry out to fully investigate your title.
★ Write down the equipment, if any, you will need.
★ Plan what area/s you will need to visit.
★ Choose a suitable day(s) to carry out your investigation. Your safety is the most important thing so don't carry out this research in an area that is known to be dangerous or on a day when the weather is bad. ⇨

> ⇨
> ★ Think about your processing techniques and how you will show the information that you have collected. If you plan on drawing field sketches, why not take a camera/camera-phone and take photos that you can use to draw a field sketch from later rather than doing it on the day.

Tourism theory

Tourist towns

Most settlements have a 'function' – something that determines its main use. Larger settlements have more than one function, while smaller ones might only have one. Some examples of settlement functions are:

- industrial town
- tourist town
- university town
- market town
- fishing port
- dormitory settlement
- commuter town.

Tourist towns are settlements where many tourists choose to visit. There are many examples of tourist towns across the UK, some attracting huge numbers of visitors annually. These include larger areas such as the Lake District, Dorset Coast, Loch Lomond and The Trossachs, and smaller settlements such as Luss, Callander, Keswick, Poole and Bournemouth. Settlements that attract high numbers of visitors are called 'honeypots'. These towns can make a lot of money from businesses that can be created around tourists and by the knock-on effects of the area becoming wealthier. However, there are a number of down-sides to such a high volume of visitors to an area.

Positive and negative effects of tourism

The effects of tourism vary from place to place, but generally the consequences of tourism in an area tend to be similar.

Positive effects

- New job opportunities for local people.
- Increased business for shops, hotels and restaurants.
- More wealth is generated in the local economy – multiplier effect.
- Increased property prices.
- Improved services such as sports and leisure facilities and transport links, for example more frequent bus services, improvements to roads.
- Less need for young people to leave the area as more job opportunities.

Negative effects

- Jobs are mainly seasonal and often low paid.
- Overcrowding of honeypot areas.

- Increased traffic congestion.
- Pollution from vehicles and water sports activities such as jet skis and boats.
- Litter problems.
- Erosion of farmland.
- Livestock can be disturbed/scared and gates may be left open allowing them to escape.
- Vandalism of local area may increase.
- Demand for second homes outprices locals.

Managing tourism
Solutions

- Educate tourists by offering leaflets, guided walks and information centres.
- Encourage people to travel by public transport rather than by car.
- Try to encourage tourists to larger settlements that can tolerate larger visitor numbers.
- Provide more bins and signs showing tourists how to properly dispose of litter.
- Zone off areas of farmland that is particularly vulnerable and build proper paths.
- Offer schemes where houses are only sold to local people.

National Parks and voluntary organisations
National Parks

There are 15 national parks in the UK – ten in England, two in Scotland and three in Wales. These areas are protected because they are considered to be areas of outstanding natural beauty. Each national park is looked after by the National Park Authority. In Scotland, the National Park Authority has four main aims:

1 To conserve and enhance the natural and cultural heritage of the area.
2 To promote sustainable use of the natural resources of the area.
3 To promote understanding and enjoyment (including enjoyment in the form of recreation) of the special qualities of the area by the public.
4 To promote sustainable economic and social development of the area's communities.

There are a number of ways that the National Park Authority tries to manage tourism within the 15 national parks:

- Refusing planning permission for any plans that may cause conflict between tourists and local people.
- Introducing traffic management schemes such as one-way systems, pedestrianisation of streets and creating no-street parking areas and building new car parks.
- Trying to attract people away from honeypot areas by advertising attractions in other areas.

- Siting Tourist Information Centres in national parks, which aim to educate visitors.
- Employing park rangers to spot and prevent problems between different types of tourists.
- Zoning of leisure activities.
- Able to insist that new houses are only sold to local people.

National Trust

The National Trust is a voluntary organisation that aims to conserve and promote the nation's treasured places and collections so that they can be enjoyed by future generations. In order to do this, the Trust has a number of areas of responsibility in Scotland, including:

- architectural wonders
- coastlines
- natural and designed landscapes and all the wildlife they contain
- 190,000 acres of countryside
- 46 Munro mountains
- 394 miles of mountain footpaths
- 10,000 archaeological sites
- seven national nature reserves
- 45 Sites of Special Scientific Interest.

The National Trust aims to minimise conflict between different land users and ensures that the land that they own is protected and not used in a way that will upset others.

Example National 5 assignment
Processed Information

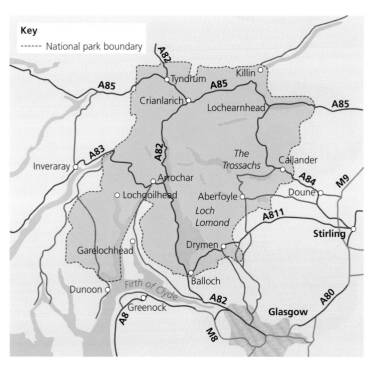

Map 1 Loch Lomond and The Trossachs National Park

Photo 1 Vehicle congestion in Luss

Photo 2 Overcrowded beach in Luss

Photo 3 Litter problems in Luss

Key
- 18–25
- 26–35
- 36–45
- 46–55
- Over 55

Chart 1 Age group of questionnaire respondents

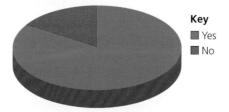

Key
- Yes
- No

Chart 2 Proportion of questionnaire respondents who were local residents

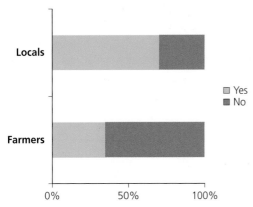

Locals

Farmers

Key
- Yes
- No

0%   50%   100%

Chart 3 Answers to question: 'Overall do tourists bring more positive effects to Luss?'

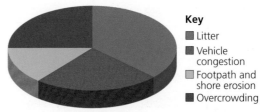

Key
- Litter
- Vehicle congestion
- Footpath and shore erosion
- Overcrowding

Chart 4 Answers to question: 'What are the main problems brought by tourism?'

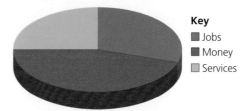

Key
- Jobs
- Money
- Services

Chart 5 Answers to question: 'What are the main benefits tourists bring to Luss?'

Table 1 Facilities found in Luss

General facilities	Recreational facilities
Shops	Water taxi
Cafés	Golf course
Restaurants	Footpaths
Hotels	Luss Hills
Bed and breakfasts	Cycle paths
Visitor centre	Play park
Primary school	Picnic area
Village hall	Pier
Pilgrimage Centre	Speed boat trips
	Cruise boat trips
	Waterskiing and canoe clubs

Table 2 Average house prices

Average house price in Luss	Average house price in Dalmally
£300,000	£168,000

National 5 Geography assignment	
Candidate name:	Joe Bloggs

State the topic or issue you have researched

The aim of my assignment was to investigate the effects of tourism on Luss.

Research methods (6 marks)

Describe two research methods you used to collect information about your topic or issue.

Location

I chose to study the small, ancient settlement of Luss, as it is a small village on the western side of Loch Lomond within the Loch Lomond and The Trossachs National Park. It is situated approximately 30 miles from Glasgow and 40 miles from Stirling. It is accessible by the A82 that continues all the way to Inverness.

1 I carried out a questionnaire

Before I began there were several things that I had to consider. First of all, I needed to think about what the purpose of the questionnaire was, for example, what exactly did I want to get from this research? The main focus of my questionnaire was to find out what the positive and negative effects of tourism are in this area. I produced a questionnaire that was easy to understand and only required the respondent to tick a box that was relevant to them. This way the questionnaire was quick and straightforward but gave me all the information that I required. My research was concerned with local residents as these are the people that are affected by tourism, so I chose to carry out this study on a weekday, when the area would be less busy, thus giving me more opportunity to speak to residents.

As Luss is only a small village, I made the decision beforehand to approach every third person, as there were not very many people on the streets. For the purpose of my research, it was not important that I focus on a specific age group or gender, as I wanted to get an overall opinion. When I approached someone I was polite and explained the purpose of the questionnaire. Then it was up to the person to fill out the form. I found that most people wanted me to tick the boxes for them.

When I had all the information that I required I was able to put my results into graph form, to make it easier to interpret. I decided to use a pie chart to show the information, as it was relatively straightforward to convert my findings into percentages based on the number of people that I asked. ⇒

2 I researched information online

There were a few things that I wanted to find out using various websites. Firstly, I wanted to identify if property prices in this area were vastly different from surrounding areas outwith the National Park boundary. In order to do this I used www.rightmove.co.uk and www.zoopla.co.uk. I compared house prices in Luss to house prices in the village of Dalmally, which is just outside the National Park boundary.

I also used www.visitscotland.com and www.loch-lomond.net to find out what facilities and attractions are found in Luss.

Conclusions (14 marks)

For this section you must:

(i) Describe and explain, in detail, the main findings of your research.

(ii) State what conclusions you have reached about your topic or issue.

Description of findings

Map 1 shows the location of Luss village, within the Loch Lomond and The Trossachs National Park. The map shows some of the settlements within the National Park and some of the larger conurbations nearby such as Stirling and Glasgow. It also shows the accessibility of Luss village via the A82.

Photographs 1–3 show some of the problems found in the village of Luss. Photograph 1 shows the problem of vehicle congestion on the narrow roads in Luss. Photograph 2 shows the problem of overcrowding on Luss beach and Photograph 3 shows the problem of litter in the village.

Charts 1–5 show the results of the questionnaire given to the selected members of the public. Chart 1 shows the age group of the people asked. The largest age category was 46–55 years, and this accounted for approximately 45 per cent of those asked, while the smallest age group was 18–25 years, who only accounted for 5 per cent of the of those asked.

Chart 2 shows the percentage of people who answered the questionnaire that were a local resident to Luss. Of those asked, 85 per cent were local residents, while 15 per cent where visiting the village. The results of Charts 3, 4 and 5 are the answers given by the local residents, not the visitors.

Chart 3 shows the opinion of local residents to tourism. They were asked, 'Overall do tourists bring more positive effects to Luss?' and 70 per cent of locals believed that tourism did bring more benefits than problems. However, 65 per cent of local farmers disagreed with this and said that they believed tourists bring more problems than positives.

Chart 4 shows the problems that local residents believe are caused by tourism. The largest category is litter problems, accounting for approximately 40 per cent of the answers, while footpath and shore erosion was the least mentioned with only 14 per cent of people considering this a problem.

Chart 5 shows the results to the question, 'What are the main benefits tourists bring to Luss?' Only three things were mentioned: 45 per cent of people answered 'money', 30 per cent of people said 'jobs' and the final benefit was 'services' mentioned by 25 per cent of respondents.

Table 1 shows the facilities found in Luss. They have been sub-categorised into general facilities and recreational facilities. Some examples of general facilities include cafés, a primary school and village hall, while the recreational facilities include footpaths, cycle paths, play park and water sports.

Finally, Table 2 shows the house prices in Luss compared to the similar sized village of Dalmally which is outside the National Park boundary.

Explanation of findings

For the purpose of my study, I asked 20 different people to take part in my questionnaire. As this is a very small village with a population of only 450 people, getting 20 people to take part took a long time. Chart 1 shows that most people taking part in the questionnaire were over 36 years of age, with the biggest age group taking part aged between 46 and 55. These results mirror the population structure of the area according to the 2011 census. Most people living in Luss are over 35 years of age, with very few young people living there. The number of young people under the age of 20 is very low for the area compared to national figures, while the number of people over the age of 45 is higher than the national average, in line with other National Park communities.

Chart 3 shows that there was a significant difference between local people and local farmers' opinions of tourism in the area, with 70 per cent of local people believing that tourism brought more positives than negatives compared to 35 per cent of local farmers. There are a number of reasons why this would be the case. Firstly, local residents' experiences of visitors to the village may be more positive as they will see the benefits that tourism brings. Benefits include more jobs being created, money being generated in the local community through increased spending and improvements being made to local services, such as increased bus services in summer months, the water taxi operating seasonally and many facilities created around tourism. All of these benefit local residents as well as tourists. While farmers identify these positives as well, they experience many negative effects of tourism that are specific to farming, such as litter being dropped in their fields and potentially causing harm to their livestock, gates being left open allowing livestock to escape and soil erosion where tourists deviate from the designated footpaths, causing land to become less fertile. All of these cause a lot of problems for farmers, including loss of income in some cases.

Chart 4 shows some of the problems brought by tourism. The four mentioned by local residents were litter problems, vehicle congestion, footpath and shore erosion and overcrowding. These tend to be the most mentioned problems when considering negative impacts of tourism in tourist areas. Popular tourist areas, like Luss, are usually very small settlements that cannot cope with high volumes of tourists. Luss is a very small village and it is renowned for its beauty and tranquility. It has been described as the 'Jewel in the Crown of Loch Lomond' and therefore huge numbers of visitors come to Luss throughout the year, but most often during the summer months. Like all popular tourist settlements, the high volumes of visitors bring many problems. The overcrowding in the village is a main concern of local residents. On busy summer days the small narrow streets and the beach can be swarmed with tourists, as shown in Photograph 2. Luss is an ancient settlement and as a result the streets are very narrow, which does not allow for many vehicles, as shown in Photo 1. Furthermore, Luss is only accessible from the A82 by the Old Military Road that passes through Luss village. There are only two other roads in the village itself. This makes vehicle congestion even worse as everybody travels into the village the same way. Litter is considered the biggest problem brought by tourists. It is inevitable that with such high volumes of visitors comes a lot of litter. Luss beach, pier, streets and play park can all be littered with crisp packets, empty cans and packaging, which is unsightly and frustrating for local residents. Some evidence of this is shown in Photograph 3.

Chart 5 shows the benefits that tourism brings to the area. The three mentioned were money, jobs and services. Money relates to the money generated by tourism in the local shops and services. The owners of these services then have increased spending power and so money is continuously injected into the local community; this is called the multiplier effect. Local residents also suggested that many jobs are created in Luss due to tourism. Some of these jobs are seasonal though, where people are only employed during the summer months. Finally, the local residents believe that local services and facilities are improved during summer months.

From Table 1 it is clear that there are a number of local services and facilities in Luss. Considering its size and population there are a very large number of facilities on offer, both general and recreational. The general services are ones that are most likely to suit local residents but are made much busier by tourists, while the recreational facilities tend to be aimed at tourists and visitors to the village. Facilities such as the water taxi, boat trips and water sports clubs are mainly operational during the summer months, for example the water taxi is available seven days a week during summer months but not at all during winter months. This shows that there is not as much need for these services during the winter when there are far fewer tourists.

Conclusion

The aim of my assignment was to investigate the effects of tourism on the village of Luss.

Overall, it is possible to conclude that tourism brings many benefits to the village of Luss and, on the whole, most people are happy with tourism in the area. However, there are a number of residents, particularly local farmers, who believe tourists bring more harm than good.

Tourists visiting the village of Luss bring a lot of money to the local community, which in turn creates more jobs and more disposable income for the local residents. A number of facilities have been created due to the high volume of tourists visiting the area, which benefits locals too.

The downside to such high volumes of visitors is the problems of litter, vehicle congestion, footpath and shore erosion and overcrowding, which many locals find frustrating.

It was useful to my study to speak to both local residents and local farmers as they had very different opinions of tourism in the local area. In the future, it might also be a good idea to include someone from the National Park Authority, as they would also have very good insight into the pros and cons of tourism in the area.

As the study was about the effects of tourism, it seemed only fair that it was only local people that were asked to complete the questionnaire. Not including the results of those questionnaires given to visitors to the village made my results more accurate and a truer reflection of the effects as it is the local people who experience these effects, both positive and negative.

Overall, it is fair to conclude that tourists bring both positive and negative effects to the village of Luss in the Loch Lomond and The Trossachs National Park.

Don't forget – you only have one hour to write up your assignment!

3.8
Population study

Choosing a title

Now that you have opted to carry out a population study, you must choose an appropriate title. For this, you must decide what exactly you want to focus on, for example, are you going to compare the population structure in two or more different areas? Are you planning to concentrate on a particular theme, such as crime rates? Or are you going to look at a specific category of people such as young families or the elderly? There is a lot to think about, so here are some ideas:

Things to consider

1 Compare the population structure in two rural areas.
2 Compare the population structure in two or more rural villages.
3 Compare the population structure of a village with a town.
4 Compare the population structure from the CBD to the suburbs.
5 Why are some villages more popular to live in than others?
6 Why are some areas more popular with families than others?
7 Why are some areas more popular with elderly people than others?
8 How do crime rates vary across the city?
9 How do house break-ins differ between urban areas?
10 How do crime rates vary between the inner city and the suburbs?

Top tip

Don't make your title too complicated otherwise you will confuse yourself and the marker.

Collecting evidence in the field

In the exam, you need to describe two research methods used to collect information about your chosen topic. However, in practice you will probably have to carry out many more and you can choose two of your 'best' for the exam.

Before you start

Before you start your population study there are several things to think about.
★ Choose a title.
★ Write down all the research methods you will need to carry out to fully investigate your title.
★ Write down the equipment, if any, you will need.
★ Plan what area(s) you will need to visit.
★ Choose a suitable day(s) to carry out your investigation. As previously mentioned, your safety is the most important thing so don't carry out this research in an area that is known to be dangerous or on a day when the weather might cause difficulties. ⇨

★ Think about your processing techniques and how you will show the information that you have collected. If you plan on drawing field sketches, why not take a camera/camera-phone and take photos that you can use to draw a field sketch from later rather than doing it on the day.

Population theory

Population of urban zones

Population of the central business district (CBD)

- This area of the city has a very low population density. The vast majority of the land use in the CBD is shops and offices. Although there are some residential properties, these are mainly flats and apartments. Very few detached or semi-detached or terraced houses are found in the CBD.
- The population structure of the CBD shows that the vast majority of people living there are young people aged 16–29. These people tend to be either students or young professionals. There are very few families and children living in the CBD and similarly there are very few elderly people living there.
- Crime rates in the CBD are the highest in the city, particular in relation to vehicle crime, violent crime, burglary and theft.

Population of the inner city

- This area of the city has the highest population density. Due to the history of the inner city being an area where there was a mixture of industry and housing, there are relatively few detached and semi-detached houses here, with the exception of more affluent areas. The main property types found here are flats and apartments.
- The population structure of the inner city is more mixed than the CBD. The inner city tends to contain some of the lowest house prices in the city and so it appeals to certain population groups such as single parents and the unemployed. There are many young people over the age of 16 living the in the inner city. These people may be attracted by the low property prices and proximity to the CBD. A relatively small number of families and elderly people tend to live in inner-city areas, although families may be found in the more affluent parts of the inner city.
- Crimes rates are lower in the inner city compared to the CBD but they are still high.

Population of the suburbs

- The suburbs have a relatively low population density. This area is almost fully residential with some small commercial properties. The majority of housing in the suburbs is detached, semi-detached or terraced housing, although there are some flats and apartments as well.

- The main category of people living in the suburbs is families. The suburbs were built with families in mind and the clean, quiet environment and number of schools found in these areas makes them very attractive to families. House prices are high in the suburbs, which is why few unemployed people or single parents are found in this area. Some elderly residents also live in the suburbs.
- Crime rates are lowest in the suburbs.

Example Higher assignment
Processed Information

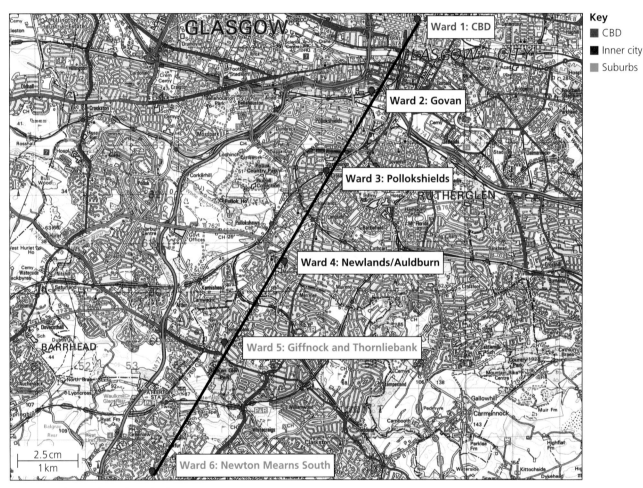

Map 1 Six electoral wards studied

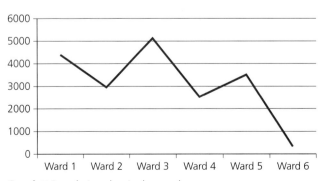

Graph 1 Population density by ward

Graph 2 Population by zone

Map extract reproduced by permission © Crown copyright 2017 Ordnance Survey 100047450.

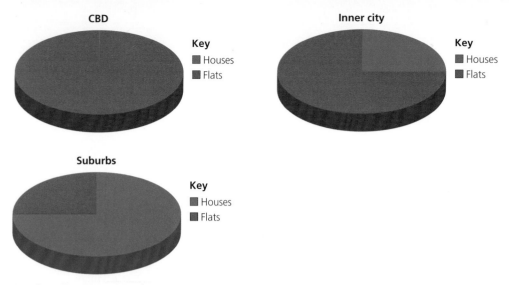

Graph 3 House type per urban zone

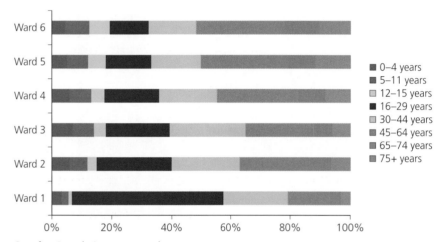

Graph 4 Population structure by age

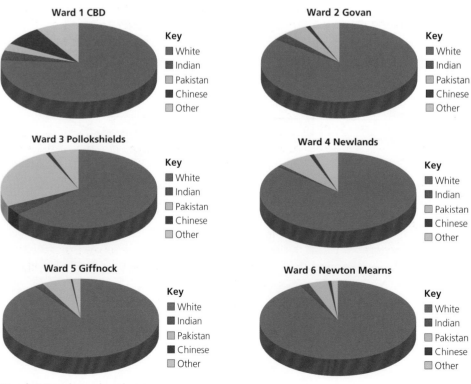

Graph 5 Population by ethnicity

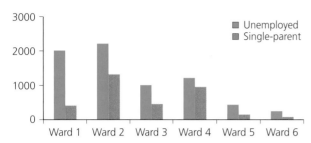

Graph 6 Number of unemployed and single-parent families per ward

Higher Geography assignment	
Candidate name:	Joe Bloggs

Introduction

Knowledge and understanding of the topic.

The aim of my assignment was to investigate how the population structure changes from the CBD to the suburbs.

In order to investigate this, I decided to look at six areas in detail, all in different parts of Glasgow from the CBD to the suburbs. Ward 1 is the Central Business District and is in the very centre of Glasgow. Ward 2 is Govan, which is an old shipbuilding area in Glasgow's inner city. Ward 3 is Pollokshields, which is another inner-city area in the south side of Glasgow. This area is mainly residential, with old tenement buildings; however, in the eighteenth and nineteenth centuries it was a mixture of industry and housing, mainly coal mining and steel works. Ward 4 is Newlands/Auldburn, which is a more affluent area in Glasgow's inner city/suburbs. It is mainly residential. Ward 5 is Giffnock and Thornliebank, located in the suburbs of Greater Glasgow. They are affluent areas that are very appealing to live in. Finally, Ward 6 is Newton Mearns which is another very wealthy area in Greater Glasgow. It is mostly residential and once again, a highly desirable area to live in.

I had an idea of what the population structures would be like in each of these wards before I conducted any research. Typically, the CBD has very few people living there as it is mainly a commercial area with shops and offices. People that do choose to live in the CBD tend to be young professionals or students who want to be close to the entertainment facilities. Housing in the CBD tends to be flats; there are very few houses in the central business district. Inner-city areas have high numbers of people living there. This is where the majority of the population will settle. The housing type can vary from flats to large detached houses and the population structure can be just as varied as young and old will live in the inner city. The suburban areas tend to be more affluent areas. Housing type tends to be large houses with gardens because land prices are lower. It is mainly families and older people who live here as these people are able to afford the house prices. For that reason, many professionals live in the suburbs.

Research methods

A description of the research methods used and/or evaluation of the usefulness and/or reliability of any technique or sources used.

I selected six areas along an urban transect from the CBD (central business district) to the suburbs, as shown in Map 1. The six zones selected are a good representation of the urban zones within the city. Ward 1 is in the CBD, Wards 2, 3 and 4 are in the inner city and Wards 5 and 6 are in the suburbs. Rather than just using the information on the specific district itself, I decided to use the entire electoral ward, as this gave me a better reflection of the areas themselves.

Research method 1: An urban land use transect

To complete this study, I chose one transect area from the CBD to the suburbs, using an Ordnance Survey map. As I am local to the south side of Glasgow, I decided to focus on this side of the river. I decided to use the route from the CBD to Newton Mearns, passing through Govan, Pollokshields, Newlands and Giffnock, and using the six wards shown in Figure 1. While selecting the areas to pass through, I wanted to make sure that I was including a range of residential areas in different zones of the city so that I would get an accurate reflection of how the population demographics change from one area to another. ⇨

I chose a route, as shown in Figure 1, and noted down the land uses along the whole transect. I used RICE-POTS for this survey, but I was not interested in all the land uses, so I selected:

R = residential with **Rt** = tenements, **Rs** = semi-detached, **Rd** = detached, **Rf** = multi-storey flats

I = industrial **O** = open space **X** = others

I added up the different land uses in each ward and turned them into percentages as shown in Graph 5.

Research method 2: Researched census/demographic information

For the same six wards I used www.glasgow.gov.uk and www.eastrenfrewshire.gov.uk, both of which are local authority websites that highlight population information by electoral ward. I was able to find out the population of each area as well as the breakdown of the population by age, sex, ethnicity, etc.

The websites also gave other useful information that might be relevant, such as average household size, property dwellings by tenure, type and size as well as economic information on the residents living there such as employment status and sector. All the information on these sites was collected from the 2011 census so I know that the information is reliable.

As my study produced a lot of unexpected results, if I was to conduct this investigation again in the future, I would use two different urban transects, one in the north of the city and one in the south. It would be interesting to see if the percentages and figures were vastly different in other areas of the city, as regeneration will not be as common in the north of the city as it is in the south.

Analysing findings

Using the Processed Information to analyse the information.

Figure 1 shows the urban transect with the six electoral wards. Ward 1 is in the central business district, Wards 2, 3 and 4 are in the inner city and Wards 5 and 6 are in the suburbs. Wards 1–4 are governed by Glasgow City Council, whereas Wards 5 and 6 fall into East Renfrewshire local authority.

Graph 1 shows the population density per ward. From this graph it appears that the population is quite erratic and does not give a downward trend, as I would have expected. For example, Ward 1 (CBD) has a high population density with over 4,000 people per km^2, it then drops to roughly 3,000 per km^2 in Ward 2 (Govan). Ward 3 is as I would have expected with a high population density of over 5,000 per km^2 before dropping to 2,500 per km^2 in Ward 4, rising again in Ward 5 (Giffnock) to 3,500 and then falling substantially to 400 per km^2 in Ward 6 (Newton Mearns South). These figures are not as I would have anticipated. I expected the population to be low in the CBD, rise in the inner city and gradually fall as you move further out of the city. In order to explain this, I had to look at each ward individually.

Ward 1 (CBD) appears to have a high population density, as the entire population of the centre is concentrated into a very small area. Of all the accommodation in the CBD, Graph 3 shows that 99 per cent of it is flats, most likely upper-storey flats that cannot be used for commercial purposes. Ward 2 (Govan) is a very large ward that incorporates many areas of the city. Tradeston and Kinning Park remain industrial areas, therefore much of the land here is used for commercial premises and factories. There are also old derelict factory buildings that have not been knocked down or regenerated so remain in these areas. The ward also includes much of the new developments along the Clydeside such as Pacific Quay, which includes the Science Centre and BBC studios, all of which contain very little housing. Bellahouston Park is located within this ward, the park itself is 0.7 km^2, which obviously takes up a huge amount of space. Regeneration in this area has been going on for several years now, and many tenement houses have been knocked down. For all these reasons, population density is quite low. Again, this was reflected in the land use survey, the results shown in Graph 5. 50 per cent of land use in Ward 2 was industrial, 25 per cent was residential and one fifth of the land was open space. Ward 3 (Pollokshields) is as I expected. It has a very high population density as this area is less industrial and mainly consists of tenement houses and high-rise flats, both of which can house high numbers of people. Graph 5 shows that 50 per cent of Ward 3 is residential. Much of the housing here is tenement flats and the ground floors are often used for commercial premises, accounting for the 30 per cent. Again, Ward 4 (Newlands) had a much lower population density than expected, because Pollok Country Park makes up almost half of the total area of this ward, with an area of 1.4 km^2. The residential areas of Newlands, Hillpark, Pollokshaws, Cathcart, Muirend and Carnwadric make up the remainder. These areas contain many tenement flats and terraced houses. Presumably, if I only looked at population density in just these areas it would actually be high. Again, this is reflected in the results of the land use survey, shown in Graph 5. 30 per cent of land uses in Ward 4 was open space, accounting for the large area of land Pollok Park covers. 55 per cent was residential and 10 per cent was industrial, mainly shops and small businesses. ⇨

Ward 5 (Giffnock) again had surprisingly high figures. There is a lot of development going on in this area, as it has become a very desirable area to live. The streets here have rows of houses, because as many properties as possible have been squeezed into a small amount of space. 65 per cent of land in Ward 5 was used for residential purposes. Mainly detached and semi-detached houses with gardens. Ward 6 (Newton Mearns South) is exactly as I anticipated. There is a very low population density here, as 75 per cent of the accommodation in the suburbs is houses; in this ward, these will be large houses with large gardens.

By looking at the population in Graph 2, it adopts the pattern that I expected, where the CBD has the lowest population, as very few people choose to live there, other than young people and students. This is followed by the suburbs, because these areas have larger houses which are more expensive and therefore less affordable for most people. Finally, the inner city has by far the largest population as this area contains the most variety of housing and is affordable for most people.

Graph 4 shows the breakdown of the population by age group. From the graph it shows that Ward 6 (Newton Mearns South) has the highest percentage of young people living there. Almost 20 per cent of the population are aged under 15. Ward 1 (CBD) has the least number of young people – approximately only 6 per cent of the CBD's population are aged under 15. Ward 1 has, by far, the highest percentage of people aged between 16 and 29 compared to Ward 6 which has very few 16–29-year-olds living there. Ward 6 has the highest percentage of 45–64-year-olds – approximately 30 per cent of the population fall into this age group, compared to Ward 1 which has very few 45–64-year-olds. Finally, Ward 5 (Giffnock) and Ward 6 (Newton Mearns South) have the highest percentage of elderly people, with approximately 10 per cent of the population in each area aged over 65.

According to Graph 4, 20 per cent of Newton Mearns South's population is under 15 and they also have the highest percentage of 45–65-year-olds. This is to be expected, as the suburbs are areas of the city where many families choose to live. These areas tend to be more affluent and have houses with gardens as opposed to the flats found in the inner city. Land prices in the suburbs tend to be lower, so it is possible to build large houses with gardens in this zone of the city. Ward 1 (CBD) has the least number of those aged under 15 years and coincidentally also has the lowest percentage of people in the 45–65 age group. This is because the CBD is not an area of the city where many people would choose to live. Land prices are very high here so large houses big enough to accommodate families are very few and far between. There are a lot of young people aged between 16 and 29 living in the CBD, because this area of the city houses student flats and halls of residence where young people studying at university will stay. Young people in this age group will happily live in the CBD, as this is where a lot of the entertainment facilities are and noise will be less of a concern to this this age group.

Conclusions

Reach a conclusion, supported by a range of evidence.

The aim of my assignment was to investigate how the population structure changes from the CBD to the suburbs.

I was surprised by the population density figures; I had expected them to follow the more 'typical' pattern of population structure in cities. Overall, the population was as I was expecting, but when I looked at the population density per ward, it did produce some anomalies. However, looking at each ward individually and understanding what is taking place in these areas, it made a lot of sense. The biggest surprise was in Ward 2, however, as regeneration has been taking place in Glasgow's inner city for many years now, but especially the south side as this is historically where much of the old industry took place. Many of the tenement flats and high rise buildings have been knocked down and replaced with more modern, two- or three-storey apartments, which house fewer people. This study has highlighted that cities are changing.

The age group of people living in the different zones of the city changes from the CBD to the suburbs. The CBD is home to mainly young people aged 16–29, while the suburbs are mainly populated by young people under the age of 15 and between the ages of 45 and 64, in other words, by families.

Ethnic minorities as well as the unemployed and single-parent families tend to live in inner-city areas as these areas tend to have the lowest house prices. These areas are appealing for these population groups as they tend to be less wealthy and so the house prices here are affordable.

Overall, it is fair to say that the population structure is very different in different zones of the city from the CBD to the suburbs, but with the changing nature of our cities, it is not possible to say that the population of the city reduces as you move out of the city.

Don't forget – you only have 1 hour and 30 minutes to write up your assignment!